LANGSTON HUGHES

—African-American Biographies—

LANGSTON HUGHES

Poet of the Harlem Renaissance

Series Consultant:
Dr. Russell L. Adams, Chairman
Department of Afro-American Studies, Howard University

Christine M. Hill

Enslow Publishers, Inc.

44 Fadem Road   PO Box 38
Box 699   Aldershot
Springfield, NJ 07081   Hants GU12 6BP
USA   UK

Library of Congress Cataloging-in-Publication Data

Hill, Christine M.
    Langston Hughes : poet of the Harlem Renaissance / Christine M. Hill.
        p.   cm. — (African-American biographies)
    Includes bibliographical references (p.   ) and index.
    Summary: Surveys the private life and literary accomplishments of the
writer whose varied works reflect the traditions, feelings, and experiences
of African Americans.
    ISBN 0-89490-815-4
    1. Hughes, Langston, 1902–1967—Biography—Juvenile literature.
2. Afro-American poets—20th century—Biography—Juvenile literature.
3. Harlem (New York, N.Y.)—Biography—Juvenile literature.
[1. Hughes, Langston, 1902–1967. 2. Poets, American. 3. Afro-
Americans—Biography.] I. Title. II. Series.
PS3515.U274Z662   1997
818'.5209—dc21
[B]   97-10991
                                                               CIP
                                                                AC

Printed in the United States of America

10 9 8 7 6 5 4 3 2

Illustration Credits: Langston Hughes Memorial Library, Lincoln University,
Pennsylvania, pp. 12, 30, 51, 57, 111; Library of Congress, pp. 34, 47, 67, 80, 84,
89; Morgan & Marvin Smith Photograph Collection, Schomberg Center, p. 6;
National Archives, pp. 105, 108; UPI/Bettmann, p. 78; UPI/Corbis-Bettmann,
p. 98; Yale Collection of American Literature, Beinecke Rare Book and
Manuscript Library, Yale University, pp. 20, 25.

Cover Illustration: Morgan & Marvin Smith Photograph Collection, Schomberg
Center.
Excerpts from COLLECTED POEMS by Langston Hughes, copyright © 1994 by
the Estate of Langston Hughes, reprinted by permission of Alfred A. Knopf, Inc.

CONTENTS

Langston Hughes

1

THE POET
LAUREATE OF
HIS RACE

Twenty-five hundred people packed the auditorium of the University of Minnesota on June 26, 1960. They had come to the closing ceremonies of the National Association for the Advancement of Colored People (NAACP) annual convention to see Langston Hughes receive the Spingarn Medal. Eighty-two-year-old Arthur Spingarn, president of the NAACP, stepped to the podium to introduce Hughes. In the forty-five-year history of the award, this was the first time a member of the Spingarn family presented it personally.

Hughes and Spingarn had been friends for almost forty years. Spingarn had served as Hughes's lawyer. A few days before, Spingarn had joined demonstrators protesting racial discrimination at a St. Paul store. He carried a placard that quoted from a Langston Hughes poem. An avid book collector, Spingarn had one of the world's largest libraries of writings by black authors worldwide.

He began his presentation by detailing Hughes's literary accomplishments. Hughes had published seven volumes of poetry, two novels, and two books of short stories. He had collected folklore, translated foreign authors, and written a two-volume auto-biography, several books of humor, and many children's books. Hughes was, Spingarn said, "the first member of his race in over a century to earn his living solely through his literary creations."[1]

Preparing to hand over the gold medal, Spingarn explained the significance of the award. It was established to be "presented annually to the man or woman of African descent and American citizenship who shall have made the highest achievement during the preceding year or years."[2] He read the official citation, which called Hughes the "Poet Laureate of the Negro Race." Then he presented his friend to the audience.

At fifty-eight, Hughes was no longer the slim, shy, handsome young man who published his first major poem in the NAACP journal, *The Crisis*. Only five feet four inches tall, he had grown stout and needed glasses. His power as a writer and speaker, however, was undiminished. The Spingarn Medal, the most prestigious honor bestowed by African Americans on one of their own, was particularly meaningful to him. He had prepared his speech carefully. He spoke from the heart on his beliefs about race and writing:

> [I can accept this], only in the name of the Negro people who have given me the materials out of which my poems and stories, plays and songs, have come; and who, over the years, have given me as well their love and understanding and support. Without them . . . there would have been no poems; without their hopes and fears and dreams, no stories; without their struggles, no dramas; without their music, no songs.[3]

His first debt, he said, was to the African-American tales and songs he had heard as a boy. Hearing the spirituals had made him appreciate the lyric beauty in the words of the common people. "There is so much richness in Negro humor, so much beauty in black dreams, so much dignity in our struggle, and so much universality in our problems," he marveled.[4] He did not understand why any African-American writer would want to reject his or her heritage, to be "just a writer."[5]

African-American humor had inspired humorists and comedians of stage and screen since the minstrels, he said. African-American dances had been America's dances since the Charleston. And, he noted, this influence did not stop at America's borders. African-American jive talk was imitated the world over. African-American music, America's greatest music, he emphasized, was loved worldwide.

So, he concluded stirringly, if an African-American artist celebrates this culture "could [he] possibly be afraid that the rest of the world will not accept it? . . . I would say to young Negro writers, do not be afraid of yourself. *You* are the world."[6]

Langston Hughes had been living his beliefs for forty years. As a teenager in a boardinghouse attic, he had first been moved to write stories "about Negroes, so true that people in far-away lands would read them—even after I was dead."[7] As a young man in his twenties, he had outraged many by taking jazz and the blues as his poetic inspiration. Later in life, he had crafted powerful political humor from the observations of the Harlem man in the street. Bebop and gospel inspired his poetry and drama in his old age. The translation of his work into dozens of languages proved his universality.

Applause rang out in Northrup Auditorium. Hughes had long wished to win the Spingarn Medal.[8] He had never married or had children. Instead, Hughes had "claimed the whole black race as his family."[9] When this family honored him, he considered it one of the greatest moments of his life.

2

A DREAMY
LITTLE BOY

In Joplin, Missouri, on February 1, 1902, James Langston Hughes was born. He was named James after his father, James Nathaniel Hughes, and Langston after his mother, Carolina ("Carrie") Mercer Langston. He would be called by his middle name all his life.

His parents had been married a little more than two years. They had already lost one son as an infant. They had met in the frontier town of Guthrie, Oklahoma, where Carrie Langston was teaching school. James Hughes had taken a homestead there, farming 160

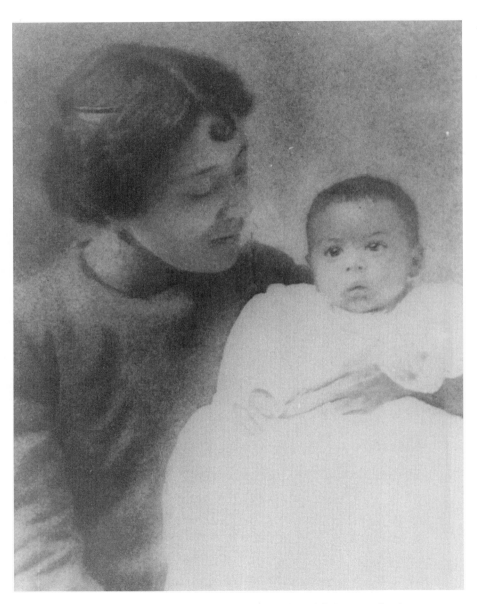

James Langston Hughes was called by his middle name after his mother, Carolina Mercer Langston.

acres. They would not stay long, however. James Hughes was an ambitious businessman and trained lawyer. Because of his race, he had been denied the opportunity to take the state bar examination to practice law. When he was offered a well-paying position with the Lincoln Mining Company in Joplin, he took it.

Living very frugally, the Hugheses saved money for James's next business ventures. Financial pressure put a strain on their marriage. James Hughes moved first to Cuba, then to Mexico to escape discrimination. In 1903, he attained the prestigious position of confidential secretary to the general manager of the American-based Pullman Company in Mexico City. The couple were having problems, so Hughes's wife and son did not accompany him on these moves. James and Carrie lived apart for two more years.

During this period, young Langston divided his time between his grandmother's home in Lawrence, Kansas, and various cities where his mother had found work. When he was five, his parents tried to reconcile. Carrie, her mother, and Langston traveled to Mexico City to reunite the family. No sooner had they arrived, though, than an enormous earthquake struck, killing hundreds. One of Langston's earliest memories was of his father carrying him to safety in the street during the quake. This was more than enough for Carrie. She immediately returned with her mother and son to the United States. The Hugheses never got together again.

When Langston was six and about to start school, his mother sent for him. She was working in Topeka, Kansas, as a stenographer for an African-American attorney. Langston left his grandmother's home to live with his mother in a room on the second floor of a downtown building. Langston kept vivid memories of that year. Their fellow tenants included a kind, elderly white architect and a young black artist. The boy was fascinated by the painter's pictures of jungle animals. Langston and his mother attended many plays and shows together. They took the train to see relatives and friends. They visited the public library. Like his mother, Langston Hughes would love the theater, travel, and books all his life.

Topeka's schools, in 1908, were segregated by race. Langston was assigned to a school across town, where most of Topeka's black citizens lived. Near his home was an all-white school. His mother, "who was always ready to do battle for the rights of a free people," appealed personally to the school board.[1] She successfully got him admitted to his neighborhood school.

This was a mixed blessing. His teacher repeatedly made cruel remarks to the class about his color. Still, young as he was, Langston noted something significant about his white teachers and classmates. Even though his own teacher was prejudiced, other white teachers were kind to him. When some white children chased him and called him names, others would stand up for him. "So I learned early not to hate *all* white people," he later wrote.[2] Still, even his prejudiced teacher was honest enough to admit that Langston was an outstanding student. She graded him "excellent" in three out of five subjects on his report card.

Langston did not remain with his mother, however. By the end of first grade, he was back in Lawrence with his grandmother. This began the most deeply influential, but saddest, period of his young life.

Langston Hughes's grandmother, Mary Patterson Leary Langston, was an extraordinary woman. She was of African, French, and Cherokee heritage. Born to a Cherokee mother, she was a free woman of color in North Carolina before the Civil War. At age nineteen, Mary survived an illegal attempt to enslave her. She escaped to Ohio, where she entered a program to prepare her for entrance to Oberlin College.

As it turned out, she never entered the college. Instead she married a handsome harness maker named Lewis Sheridan Leary in 1858. During their brief marriage, the young couple were militant abolitionists, opposing slavery. They acted as conductors on the Underground Railroad, smuggling escaped slaves to freedom in the North. The next year, the twenty-four-year-old Leary rode off one night without telling his wife—who was pregnant with their daughter, Loise—where he was going. He never returned.

Leary had joined the followers of John Brown, the radical abolitionist. In 1859 Brown and a band of anti-slavery raiders, including Leary, attacked the United States arsenal at Harper's Ferry, a town in the mountains of what is now West Virginia. The group wanted to seize weapons with which to start a massive slave rebellion. Leary was killed in the attack. Brown and the rest of his men were captured, tried, and hung for treason. Leary's blood-stained shawl, rent with bullet holes, was returned to his widow. Mary wrapped herself and, years later, her grandson Langston in this shawl. When she died she left it to him, and Hughes cherished it.

Mary's second husband, Charles Langston, was just as ardent a champion of African-American rights as her first. In marrying him, Mary became part of one of the nation's most extraordinary African-American families, the Langstons. Charles Langston's father, Ralph Quarles, was a wealthy Virginia planter. He had been ostracized from white society for living with his black housekeeper, Lucy Langston, a former slave, as if they were married. He left all his property to Lucy and their children when he died. For their own safety, his sons left Virginia when they grew up. All three went to Oberlin, Ohio, and attended college there. The eldest, Gideon, became a businessman in that state.

The youngest, John Mercer, became an attorney, law school dean, college president, ambassador to Haiti, and United States congressman from Virginia. He was one of the best-known African Americans of the nine-teenth century.

The middle son, Charles, was a militant abolitionist. He was a leader of the daring slave rescue known as the Oberlin-Wellington Raid. After the Civil War, he was active in Republican politics. He edited an African-American newspaper, in which he continued to demand equal rights and education. He and Mary married in 1869. They had two children, Nathaniel (named after Nat Turner, who led the most famous slave revolt) and Carrie. They also had a foster son, Desalines.

Though a leader of the African-American community of Lawrence, Charles Langston left little money when he died. When his widow, Mary, took their grandson Langston in, she was desperately poor. Though Mary owned her home, it was mortgaged. Most of her money went to pay off the loan. Her entire income came from taking in boarders. Her first daughter, Loise, was long dead. Her son Nathaniel had been killed in a mill accident in 1897. Carrie and Desalines had little to spare. Mary was too old and proud to work as a servant, as most of Lawrence's African-American women did.

Still, she gave her grandson Langston a priceless gift as she raised him—an extraordinary sense of racial pride and destiny. She inspired him with her vision of the man she wished him to become. Night after night, she would take Langston on her knee and tell him stories, true stories of African-American heroism. Or she would read to him from the Bible, from fairy tales, from African-American authors like Paul Lawrence Dunbar and W.E.B. Du Bois, from newspapers and magazines. By reading to him, both his mother and grandmother gave Langston the gift of great literature at an early age.

As his grandmother aged, however, young Langston became increasingly lonely.[3] Always a quiet woman, Mary retreated into silence, spending hours rocking in her chair next to the stove. She made Langston come home immediately after school and stay inside. She did this to keep him from being hurt by Lawrence's growing segregation and racial discrimination. One of Hughes's saddest childhood memories was of hearing boys outside playing ball late one afternoon as he sat inside. "For the first time," he wrote, "loneliness strikes me, strikes me terribly, settling down in a dull ache round about, in the dusk."[4]

Carrie Hughes traveled a great deal during this period, searching for better-paying work. She lived in Colorado for a while. Langston thrilled to the sight of the Rockies when he joined her during summer vacation. More often she worked in various Kansas cities. Langston saw his mother on weekends when she lived nearby. They would attend plays or visit relatives together. Often he cried and begged his mother to keep him with her. He longed to live with her all the time, rather than with his grandmother in Lawrence. It was at this point that Langston increasingly sought refuge in books. He took strength from them to block the loneliness, hurt, and anger he felt at his grandmother's silence and his mother's absence.[5]

Langston's teachers and friends found him to be a courteous and well-behaved child. Still, he showed his angry feelings at his beloved mother publicly at least twice. Carrie Hughes loved amateur theatricals and often gave recitations at church socials. On one such occasion, she was to give the famous speech "The Mother of the Gracchi." Langston and another boy were silently to portray her sons. Instead, while she recited, Langston made faces at the people in the audience, who laughed loudly. For this, he got the worst spanking of his life. Yet, soon after, he deliberately "forgot" a poem he knew perfectly and was to recite at a Children's Day program. In the audience was his mother, who had come all the way from Kansas City to hear him.

He continued to excel in racially mixed classes. Then, in seventh grade, he was assigned to a white teacher who isolated the African-American students in a separate row. In his autobiographical novel, *Not Without Laughter,* Hughes described a similar incident.

Langston Hughes as a young boy. From ages six to thirteen, he lived with his elderly grandmother in Lawrence, Kansas.

His fictional hero, Sandy, responded by fighting back tears. Not Langston. Like his mother and his grandparents, who were not afraid to fight for equal rights, the young man fought back. He defiantly made signs to prop on each desk in the segregated seats. The signs read "Jim Crow Row." (The laws that then required segregation were called Jim Crow laws.) When the teacher tried to remove the signs, Langston ran into the schoolyard shouting that the teacher had a Jim Crow row.[6] Parents complained and the segregated seating was stopped.

Mary Langston occasionally rented out her entire house and moved in, along with her grandson, with close friends, the Reeds. This warm and loving childless African-American couple provided Langston with the happiest family atmosphere he was to know. These kind people gave him a home in 1915 when his grandmother suddenly died. Langston was thirteen. He did not cry on that day, he wrote, because something about his grandmother's stories of heroism told him not to.[7] Her house went to the mortgage man.

Although he loved the Reeds, Langston was eager to live again with his mother, who had remarried. Langston greatly liked his new stepfather, Homer Clark, a chef. He was delighted that Homer's son, Gwyn, would be his stepbrother. The Clarks sent for Langston in the summer of 1915. He joined his mother and stepfather in their new home in Lincoln, Illinois.

Eighth grade in Lincoln's Central School was a triumph for Langston. There he was one of only two African-American students. He was popular among his white classmates and esteemed by his white teachers. One of them described him as "standing intellectually head and shoulders above the group."[8] He was chosen class poet. With the assignment of praising the graduating eighth graders at commencement, Langston wrote his first poem. It was a great success.

His new home was no more stable than his previous ones, however. His mother and stepfather continued to move regularly, in search of better jobs. Their next stop was Cleveland, Ohio, in 1916. Homer Clark had found a good job in a steel mill there as America was about to enter World War I.

This gave Langston a wonderful opportunity to attend an outstanding secondary school, Cleveland's Central High School. He made the most of it. The school had excellent teachers, high academic standards, many extracurricular activities, and a diverse student body. It provided an intellectually and socially stimulating environment in which the young man could begin his development as a writer.

At the end of Langston's sophomore year, the Clarks separated. His mother found a job in Chicago, where Langston joined her. He worked for the summer as an elevator operator. Then his mother demanded that he quit school and work full-time to help support her and little Gwyn. When Sandy in *Not Without Laughter* faced the same dilemma, he was saved by money provided by his aunt. The real Langston did not have such a fairy godmother. He returned to Cleveland alone and attended high school while living by himself in a boardinghouse. A burning desire for education led him to this unusual living arrangement.

At Central, teachers and classmates saw a smiling, handsome, self-assured scholar. He ran track, drilled other students in military training, was elected to the student council, and was an officer and member of numerous clubs. At night, alone in a rented attic room, Langston read philosophy and literature. He also began to write poetry and stories. Dozens of them were published in the school's literary magazine. A favorite English teacher had opened the world of modern poetry to him. She assigned contemporary poets as class reading. Hughes's favorite poet as a teenager was Carl Sandburg. He also loved Walt Whitman, who would remain a lifelong inspiration.

At the end of his junior year, his mother and stepfather reconciled. They moved back to Cleveland and took Langston in. Then, completely unexpectedly, Langston received a message from his father. A letter arrived saying that James Hughes would be passing through Cleveland. On his way back from business in New York, he would pick his son up. "You are to accompany me to Mexico for the summer," he wrote.[9]

3

HURRY UP

"A s mean and evil a Negro as ever lived!"[1] That was how Carrie Hughes described her ex-husband. Young Langston could not believe this. He pictured his father as a strong brown cowboy in a sombrero, riding proud and free between his ranch and businesses in Mexico. There James Hughes would not have the restrictions the United States placed on an African American of his talent and ambition in 1919. Langston would soon find out which view was correct.

James Nathaniel Hughes was forty-eight years old

Langston Hughes's father, James Nathaniel Hughes, Jr.

when he reunited with his only son. James's father, born a slave, had finished his life as a respected farmer and church official in Indiana. Two of James's brothers had ridden the frontier with the legendary African-American "Buffalo Soldiers" of the United States Cavalry. Both of his grandfathers had been white. While living in Mexico, James Hughes became quite successful. He was fluent in Spanish and German. He practiced law, dealt in real estate, and negotiated business deals in Mexico's international business community.

Langston was looking forward to getting to know his father, as well as to traveling to another country. Just before James Hughes was to pick up his son, Langston and his family moved. Every day Langston returned to their old home looking for mail stating his father's time of arrival. As he had feared, the message went astray. For a time, Langston thought they had missed each other. In a panic, he checked Cleveland's hotels for African Americans.[2] Hurrying to one that had a James Hughes registered, Langston passed a short bronze man on the street. The two sensed something about each other and both turned to stare. "Are you Langston?" the man asked. Why had his train not been met? he demanded without a word of greeting. When Langston explained that he had missed the telegram, James Hughes snarled, "Just like niggers. Always moving."[3]

James Hughes continued to disown his race during the trip. "Look at the niggers," he said disdainfully when he saw African-American farm workers from the train window.[4] It did not take Langston long to realize he had made a terrible mistake. "That summer in Mexico was the most miserable I have ever known," he stated flatly. "I did not like my father."[5] "My father hated Negroes," he said. "I think he hated himself, too, for being a Negro."[6]

James Hughes lived in the high mountain valley town of Toluca. It was a beautiful, lush, flower-filled setting in the shadow of a volcano. His home, at the edge of a park, was comfortable. It had a stable and a flock of chickens, as well as a housekeeper and servant boy.

Langston's visit was not intended to be a vacation, however. His father set him to the tasks of mastering bookkeeping, typing, and Spanish grammar. Every day his father gave Langston a set of exercises to do. Then he berated his son when they were not done well or fast enough. "Hurry up. Hurry up" was his constant rebuke.[7] Nothing could be done fast enough for James Hughes. Langston's father drove himself mercilessly and expected everyone else to do the same. He was also just as frugal as he had been when he was married to Langston's mother.

Near the end of the summer, James Hughes told his son that he would take him along on a business trip to Mexico City. While there, they would attend the bullfights and visit the beautiful floating gardens of Xochimilco. On the day of their departure, they arose in the frigid dark at 4:30 A.M. This way they would arrive at the station early enough to get seats. James Hughes could have spent more money to get reserved seats, but he had chosen not to. As they gulped down their breakfast, Hughes suddenly demanded, "Hurry up," and something in Langston snapped.[8]

His stomach turned, his body shook and burned. He was overcome with a desire to hit his father. Instead, he turned around and went back to bed. His father asked him what was the matter. Was he was still going with him to Mexico City? When Langston answered no, James Hughes left without him.

Langston's inward-turned anger had made him physically ill.[9] Four days later, his father found him still weak and feverish. He took Langston by train to the hospital. There, Langston found out it was costing his father twenty dollars a day (a great sum of money for that time). He was in no hurry to recover. By the time he was discharged, it was almost September.

Alone, Langston headed back to Cleveland. In San Antonio, Texas, Langston made sleeping car reservations in Spanish for the next leg of his journey. The railway employee, apparently believing him to be Mexican, issued the ticket. He did not put Langston in the segregated African-American car, which had no sleeping berths. At breakfast, his white tablemate rose, literally screaming, when he realized he was seated with an African American. A clerk in St. Louis, Missouri, refused to serve Langston an ice-cream soda because of his race. "I knew I was home in the U.S.A.," Langston noted ironically.[10]

Back at Cleveland's Central High School, Langston was one of the best-liked and most accomplished seniors. "Everyone adored him," a classmate remembered.[11] He was nominated for class president, though he did not win. He competed in track and the high jump, acted in the school play, and was named class poet and yearbook editor. He continued to write and publish in the school magazine.

He graduated with honors in June 1920. Most of his friends had been accepted to college, but Langston had not yet applied to any. One of his teachers wrote to him, wondering if the relatively liberal Central High had prepared him for the racism he would encounter in the wider world. The teacher knew how much Langston would have to overcome to achieve what he was capable of. The well-meaning teacher had underestimated the obstacles already overcome by Langston. He had also misjudged the seemingly easygoing young man. Langston already knew exactly what he was going to do and how.

As a student, he had already determined his goal. He wanted to be a writer. He wanted to write about the

Langston Hughes was a member of the Cleveland Central High School relay team, which won the city championships two years in a row. He was also one of the most popular and accomplished students in the class of 1920.

African-American people. To do this he would need an education. He would need to be immersed in an African-American community. He had decided to go to New York City, specifically Harlem, renowned as "the greatest Negro city in the world."[12] He planned to attend Columbia University. His father's recent letters had hinted that he might be willing to finance his son's college education. To fulfill this dream, Langston was prepared first to return to Mexico and deal with James Hughes.

On the train ride south, a melancholy Langston observed the sun setting across the Mississippi River. He thought of that river's sad role in slavery times, when slaves were sent by water to the slave market in New Orleans.[13] Then he thought of the role other rivers played in African history—the Nile, the Congo. He began to write a poem, "The Negro Speaks of Rivers." It would become his first published poem for adults and one of his most famous. He was only eighteen years old.

James Hughes was somewhat more pleasant that summer. He had a new housekeeper, Bertha Schultz, who was a German war widow. Langston's Spanish had improved to the point where he could try to read Spanish literature and make friends among the young men of the town.

By this time, Langston could ride and shoot well. His father arranged for them to accompany a heavily armed convoy of property owners traveling to their mountain ranches and mines. Earlier that year, James Hughes's ranch had been attacked and stripped. Hughes himself had been robbed on another journey. The country was beautiful, and James Hughes was so relaxed that he began to share his thoughts about Langston's future.

He had decided that Langston should study mining engineering to be ready to profit when the silver mines near the ranch reopened. Furthermore, he should go to college in Switzerland and attend graduate school in Germany. Langston, whose poorest subject was math, did not like this plan.

Langston insisted that he wanted to be a writer and go to Columbia University. His father challenged him to name one black writer who made any money. Langston suggested Alexandre Dumas, the French and African author of *The Three Musketeers*. But that was in Europe, his father countered, where there was no color line.[14] The discussion ended. Tension between them resumed. James Hughes refused to send Langston either to college or back home until he submitted to his wishes. Langston had no money of his own. He would be trapped for a year.

Still, he worked at his writing. For years, Langston had subscribed to *The Crisis*. Its editor was the distinguished scholar and civil rights activist W.E.B. Du Bois, whom Langston deeply admired. In 1919,

Du Bois founded a magazine for African-American children, *The Brownies' Book*. Langston sent a poem to the magazine.

The editor, Jessie Fauset, accepted it immediately. Soon, every issue contained his writing: stories, sketches, poems, a play. When he sent her "The Negro Speaks of Rivers," she accepted it immediately for publication in *The Crisis*. A few months later, *The Crisis* asked him to prepare a full page of poems. Du Bois himself was impressed with the young man's work.[15]

When his poems were published, Langston showed them to his father. James Hughes asked two questions: How long had they taken to write and how much had he been paid? Unfortunately, he had been paid nothing. Still, not long after that James Hughes changed his mind. He would, he said, pay for one year's study at Columbia. Langston applied and was accepted. When Langston and his father said good-bye at the train station in August of 1921, they did not know that they would never see each other again.

As thrilled as he was to be in New York, Langston did not like Columbia.[16] He was immediately snubbed because of his race: The college tried to deny him a dormitory room even though he had reserved it from Mexico. Few students befriended him. The college newspaper, for which he wanted to write, insultingly assigned him to social news. The editors knew that an African-American student would not even be admitted

W.E.B. Du Bois was the editor of *The Crisis* when Langston Hughes's poem "The Negro Speaks of Rivers" was published.

to the dances and fraternity events they would send him to cover.

So Langston made the most of his time by soaking up New York's color and variety. He attended lectures and readings at the Harlem Branch of the New York Public Library. He saw dozens of Broadway shows. He met the staff of *The Crisis* and began socializing with the African-American artists and intellectuals drawn to New York as the twenties dawned. Meanwhile, he came to a decision. Although his grades were good, he would leave college at the end of the year. He was not done educating himself, but he would not do it in a cold, Ivy League institution. He would travel the world and live among black people.

4

I LET DOWN
MY NETS

Langston Hughes decided first to work. After a long search, he found hard, exhausting work on a Staten Island, New York, vegetable farm. In 1922 it seemed that he would not even be considered for any job he saw advertised unless the ad specifically said "colored." "Experience was proving my father right," he noted ruefully.[1]

Shortly before Langston left Columbia, James Hughes had suffered a stroke in Mexico. Nursed by his housekeeper, Bertha Schultz, whom he would marry two years later, Langston's father made a good recovery. He and Langston continued to write letters. James Hughes even sent him money, hoping he might return to college. Langston sent the money back. His father stopped writing. For a while, Langston sent letters, then a Christmas gift, without reply. Finally, he, too, stopped. They would exchange only a handful of letters during the rest of their lives. After James Hughes's death, Langston Hughes found all the letters he had written filed carefully away among his father's possessions.

Farm work was followed by a stint as a florist's delivery man. After another frustrating job search, Hughes had a different idea. For such low wages, he might as well get to travel. So he got a job as a mess boy, or kitchen helper, on a rusty old freighter. He was so excited by the prospect of travel that he forgot to ask the ship's destination. To his disappointment, he found out that it would merely be serving as a residence for sailors in a fleet of worn-out World War I vessels.[2] They were to be laid up on the Hudson River near West Point, New York.

Finally, Hughes shipped out on another freighter. This time it had a destination, "the great Africa of my dreams," as Hughes recalled.[3] When the *West Hesseltine* sailed past New Jersey's Sandy Hook lighthouse on the night of June 13, 1923, Langston Hughes made a symbolic gesture. He dumped a box of books into the sea, telling himself that he had renounced the fantasy

worlds in them. He would embrace only the real
world, as a sailor and a writer. He saved one book—
Walt Whitman's *Leaves of Grass*, as a symbol of the poet
he still intended to be.[4]

The ship made port two weeks later at Dakar in
Senegal. Hughes was overwhelmed. "My Africa,
Motherland of the Negro peoples!" he rejoiced.[5]
The tropical beauty of the land stunned him, as did
the Africans. "People, black and beautiful as the
night," he remembered.[6]

At first, he saw things as an outsider. Despite his
appreciation of their beauty, he sometimes laughed
at the people. He wrote to his mother about the
humorous hodgepodge of clothing they wore, "from
overcoats to nothing."[7] Hughes quickly saw the
economic burden that colonialism placed on the
Africans. All fifteen coastal West African nations he
visited, with the exception of Liberia, were then
colonies of European nations. This meant that they
were ruled by countries like England, France, and
Belgium, who also controlled their economies. The
Europeans took away African wealth in the form of raw
materials and returned next to nothing. During the
months of the cruise, copra, palm oil, cocoa beans,
mahogany logs, ginger, and pepper were loaded onto
Hughes's freighter. Machinery, tools, canned goods,
and Hollywood films were unloaded.

He saw how the economic exploitation of Africans

paralleled the economic situation of African Americans in the United States, particularly in the South. This gave him an even stronger sense of brotherhood with them. Strangely, the Africans did not return his feelings. They did not consider mixed-race African Americans like Hughes to be black. Hurt though he was by this rejection, it did not affect his writing.[8] The poems Hughes composed during the voyage are filled with his identification with Africa. "Night coming tenderly / Black like me" is a famous line from one of his poems of this period.[9]

His work as a ship's messboy was very easy. The *West Hesseltine* had taken on an entire African crew in addition to its own. Americans were not supposed to be up to laboring in the African heat. Hughes doubted that it was any hotter than Chicago in the summer. During their stops at thirty-two ports, he saw as much of each country as he could. He talked to many Africans. He later wrote to some of them and sent them copies of *The Crisis*.

At the end of September, the ship headed home. The crew, which had been drunken and rowdy throughout the voyage, had become completely uncontrollable. When the *West Hesseltine* reached New York, the entire crew was fired.

Hughes soon shipped out again, this time on a freighter bound for Rotterdam, the Netherlands. There he spent a pleasant Christmas 1923, taken home for a holiday dinner by a friendly dock watchman. The weather was fierce with winter gales both to and from Europe. A second treacherous crossing to Rotterdam and a series of shipboard misfortunes led him to believe the voyage was jinxed.

He jumped ship and made his way to Paris, arriving at the city railway station with only a few dollars left. He hopped on a bus marked "L'Opera," which he knew was in the center of Paris. As the snow fell and he got out at the opera house, one famous Parisian landmark after another appeared before him. Hughes was thrilled.[10]

To stay there, though, he would need a cheap place to live and a job. He met a young woman, a Russian dancer, who was in the same situation. They pooled their money and moved in together for a while. Next, he looked for other African Americans in Paris to get leads on jobs. Rayford Logan, a former World War I officer who had remained in France, gave him a tip. There was an opening for an assistant cook in a well-known nightclub called the Grand Duc. Hughes took the job.

Appearing at the club was the haughty, beautiful, African-American singer known as Florence. After the regular customers had departed, her husband and other African-American musicians would arrive from the clubs where they worked. Then they would play for their own enjoyment until dawn. Hughes drank in the superb jazz these artists created. He had already mined the blues, an earlier form of African-American music, for poetic inspiration. Now he began to experiment with the more sophisticated rhythms of the still new and developing jazz form.

One day, Rayford Logan asked Hughes to carry a note to someone in another, more exclusive part of Paris. When he arrived at the given address, Hughes found a beautiful, cultured, English-educated young woman of African and Scotch ancestry. Her name was Anne-Marie Coussey. She had read his poetry in *The Crisis* and was delighted to meet him. She began inviting him often to tea. They went dancing and to the theater. As a beautiful Parisian spring bloomed in 1924, they fell in love.

They began to talk of marriage. When Coussey questioned his aimless Parisian existence, however, Hughes did not like it. He wanted to be loved for himself, not his education or accomplishments. While he fully intended to return to college, he wanted to grow in other ways and educate himself on his own timetable. The two decided to part. "And because her skin is the brown of an oak leaf in autumn, but a softer color, / I want to kiss her," he wrote around this time in "Fascination."[11]

When the Grand Duc closed for August vacation, Hughes spent a month touring Italy. Disaster struck on the journey back to France. Hughes's pocket was picked and all his money, along with his passport, was stolen. He could not reenter France without it. He had to exit the train at the seaside border city of Genoa. There his only hope was to wait for a merchant vessel that would agree to give him passage in exchange for work without pay.

For two desperate weeks, he took odd jobs and slept in a homeless shelter. Ship after American ship came and went, refusing to accept an African-American seaman. The desperation of this period led him to produce one of his most famous poems, "I, Too."

> *I am the darker brother.*
> *They send me to eat in the kitchen*
> *When company comes,*
> *But I laugh,*
> *And eat well,*
> *And grow strong.*[12]

When a ship with an all-black crew put into port and took him on, he was returning to a different New York. The 1920s had brought comparative prosperity and a new optimism to the African-American community. The fine arts, as well as nightlife and glamour, were flourishing. The Harlem Renaissance had begun. It was time for Langston Hughes to return and take his place as one of its stars.

5

WHEN HARLEM WAS IN VOGUE

angston Hughes returned from Europe in November 1924. A few days later, at a party in his honor, Hughes shyly took his place at the center of the new movement. The party was attended by the cream of Harlem's younger literary and intellectual crop. One of the guests was Charles S. Johnson, the African-American editor of the new magazine *Opportunity*. Johnson believed that Hughes, more than any other writer, "completely symbolized the new emancipation of the Negro mind."[1]

Arna Bontemps, a poet, met Hughes at this gathering. The two men soon became close friends. "He was the honored guest," Bontemps wrote. "Some of the most enduring of his poems had been printed in *The Crisis* in his absence, but clearly he had little knowledge of their impact. . . . With ease and apparent pleasure, he was drawn into a chair and asked what he had been doing and writing while away. He . . . began reading from his notebook the sea pieces of his voyages and the jazz poems he had written."[2] Bontemps and several others walked Hughes home. Despite the November chill, they lingered talking to him. "We forgot the cold when first one and then another recalled the poem by him that they liked best."[3]

Hughes soon learned what had been going on during his travels. In March 1924, while Hughes was still in Paris, an extraordinary party had been given in New York by Charles S. Johnson. "A small but representative group" of influential white writers, editors, publishers, and businessmen had dinner with "an equally representative group of Negroes."[4] Racially mixed social events were very rare at this time in the United States.

It was Johnson's ingenious plan to let African-American writers meet and mingle socially with the literary establishment. The white publishing world, he suspected, had no idea of the extent of literary talent among educated African Americans. He was right. Since 1905, only a handful of books by African

Americans had been published. During the later 1920s, dozens more would appear, some the direct result of this event.

Present at the party were Hughes's mentors Jessie Fauset and W.E.B. Du Bois. Also in attendance were the poets Countee Cullen and James Weldon Johnson. Excited white editors stayed late discussing literature with their black counterparts. As a result, new publishing outlets in white periodicals became available. In addition, *Opportunity*, *The Crisis*, and other black magazines showcased young authors.

African-American writers elsewhere in the United States were electrified. As to a field of dreams, they came to Harlem. "Harlem the beautiful," Arna Bontemps called it. "It was like a foretaste of paradise. A blue haze descended at night and with it strings of fairy lights on the broad avenues."[5] All-black shows were Broadway hits. Black jazz and black dances like the Charleston were all the rage among whites. Harlem nightclubs drew white customers for their fabulous music and lavish floor shows. Racially mixed dinner parties became not only possible but stylish among the elite.

Despite his new fame, Hughes was without a place to live. He moved to Washington, D.C., to join his mother and stepbrother. He hoped to arrange for a scholarship or loan to attend Howard University there. Meanwhile, Hughes took low-paying jobs in a laundry and an oyster house. He was never ashamed to earn an honest living. He also worked briefly for Carter G. Woodson, the scholar who is known as the father of African-American history.

His literary chance came when *Opportunity* announced a contest, with cash prizes, for African-American writers. The awards banquet to announce the winners was in May 1925. It was "the greatest gathering of black and white literati ever assembled in one room."[6] Before this audience of distinguished writers and representatives of the leading publishing houses, Langston Hughes was named winner of the first prize in poetry. The award was for his jazz-inflected "The Weary Blues." James Weldon Johnson read the winning poem beautifully.

> *With his ebony hands on each ivory key*
> *He made that poor piano moan with melody.*
> *O Blues!*
> *Swaying to and fro on his rickety stool*
> *He played that sad raggy tune like a musical fool.*
> *Sweet blues!*[7]

Most prominent among his admirers at the banquet was the best-selling novelist Carl Van Vechten. This white writer was a famous Roaring Twenties party giver and nightclub crawler. He was also a serious student of African-American culture and would be a

Carl Van Vechten was a best-selling novelist and notorious Roaring Twenties party giver who arranged for the publication of Langston Hughes's first book. The two remained friends for forty years.

generous promoter of Hughes's art. Van Vechten asked whether Hughes had enough poems written to fill a book. Hughes said he had. Van Vechten invited him to visit his home the very next day and bring his manuscripts. Two days later, after the men had discussed some revisions, Van Vechten promised to find a publisher for Hughes.

Within a few weeks, Van Vechten had secured a contract for Hughes with his own distinguished publisher, Alfred A. Knopf. He had also sold several Hughes poems to the fashionable magazine *Vanity Fair.* Hughes was dazzled and grateful. "How quickly it's all been done! Bravo to you!" he wrote to Van Vechten.[8]

Before the book's publication, however, Hughes still needed to make a living. No scholarship to Howard University had been offered to him. While working as a busboy at a Washington hotel, he seized an unexpected opportunity for good publicity. This was a skill he would hone throughout his life. The famous white poet Vachel Lindsay was staying at the hotel to give a poetry reading. Hughes slipped him a note and three poems along with his breakfast. Lindsay knew talent when he saw it. He announced to his audience that he had discovered a poet working in that very hotel. He read to them from Hughes's work. The next day photographs of the "busboy poet" appeared in the Washington papers.

The next month, his book, called *The Weary Blues*, was published. Reviews generally called him a promising poet, "well worth watching."[9] Other reviews praised his musicality and "understanding of the Negro heart."[10] Hughes immediately began to receive invitations to read his poems. At a reading in Cleveland, former teachers and classmates at Central High marveled at his performance.[11]

Hughes received an interest-free college loan from an admirer of his poetry, Amy Spingarn, Arthur's sister-in-law. He entered Lincoln University, near Oxford, Pennsylvania, in February 1926. He was delighted with Lincoln's picturesque rural campus. He valued its academic seriousness, its informal atmosphere, and the camaraderie of its all-male student body. It was a sociable college dominated by sports, clubs, and fraternities. Hughes joined Omega Psi Phi. As part of his initiation to the fraternity, he had to dance the Charleston while "The Weary Blues" was recited. Hughes took it with good humor.

That fall, as his sophomore year at Lincoln began, Hughes assembled a new group of poems and submitted it to Knopf. This collection, titled *Fine Clothes to the Jew*, is now considered by many scholars to be Hughes's greatest poetic achievement. It was written almost entirely in the style of the blues, raising the language of the African-American common people to pure poetry. In "Homesick Blues," he wrote,

De railroad bridge's
A sad song in de air.
De railroad bridge's
A sad song in de air.
Ever time de trains pass
I wants to go somewhere.[12]

In 1927, however, critical reaction was generally negative. Few white reviewers understood his innovative use of language. The African-American press was outraged. Among most educated African Americans, the blues was considered trash. Black reviewers characterized his book as reeking, disgusting, unsanitary, and repulsive.[13]

Hughes had already expressed his view on African-American language and art in his landmark essay "The Negro Artist and the Racial Mountain." Some African-American critics did not want art that depicted the "lower class" of black folk. "This is the mountain standing in the way of any true Negro art in America—this urge within the race toward whiteness," Hughes asserted.[14] "How difficult it would be," he went on, for such a snobbish critic "to interest himself in interpreting the beauty of his own people. He is never taught to see that beauty. He is taught rather not to see it, or if he does, to be ashamed of it."[15]

Then, with a blast, he stated his own artistic beliefs. "We younger Negro artists who create now intend to

Langston Hughes loved his years at Lincoln University, then all black and all male. Here, a relaxed Hughes waits for a train at the university railroad station.

express our individual dark-skinned selves without fear or shame. If white people are pleased we are glad. If they are not, it doesn't matter. . . . If colored people are pleased we are glad. If they are not, their displeasure doesn't matter either."[16]

Even the title of his second book, *Fine Clothes to the Jew*, was controversial. When poor African Americans needed quick money, they would take their valuables to a pawnbroker, often Jewish in those days. They would receive a loan, while their valuables were held as security. The title expressed the desperation of someone so poor that he had to pawn his clothes in an emergency. Nevertheless, many people were offended. Hughes thought the title may have contributed to the book's poor sales.[17]

That year, Hughes was introduced to a seventy-one-year-old widow from New York City. The wealthy, white Mrs. Charlotte Osgood Mason was known to be a generous patron of black artists. Hughes was intrigued.

6

To Write for a Living

"I found her instantly one of the most delightful women I had ever met, witty and charming, kind and sympathetic," he wrote.[1] Old enough to be his grandmother, Mrs. Mason showered him with praise. She was so different from his own, very reserved, grandmother. She provided encouragement in his writing and the promise of financial security. His own family had given him neither. He gave himself up to the rewards of fulfilling Mrs. Mason's plans for him.

At first, she merely slipped him gifts of money

from time to time. After six months, however, they entered into a formal agreement. Hughes would receive a monthly stipend of $150 (a generous sum in 1927). It was his to spend or to save. In return, he would provide her with a written monthly financial accounting. He would also send her frequent letters and keep up his creative writing. He was to address her as "Godmother," a name reserved for her special protégés. Hughes was satisfied with this arrangement. Being rich and white, she must truly value him for himself, he reasoned.[2] In addition, having grown up mostly among whites, Hughes believed he could read their motives accurately.[3]

Hughes now entered the most luxurious period of his life. Weekends were no longer spent at college, but on Park Avenue. Expensively dressed in evening clothes, he escorted Mrs. Mason to concerts and plays. His friendships with fellow students and writers diminished. He also wrote very little. He admitted to writing only when he was most unhappy, and this was a very happy period of his life.[4]

Mrs. Mason urged him to write a novel. Although longer literary forms generally did not appeal strongly to him, he agreed for her sake to try it.[5] In 1928, during the summer after his junior year of college, Hughes stayed alone at Lincoln University to begin writing. He planned to write a semiautobiographical novel, based on his Kansas boyhood. It was painful to recall the sorrows of his lonely childhood, but the rush of sad emotions gave him the creative push he needed.[6] When the first draft was complete, Mrs. Mason read it promptly. She was pleased but sent him pages of detailed criticism.

After a year and a half of patronage, strains began to appear in their relationship. Hughes omitted a figure in his monthly accounting and was scolded. At Christmas, she did not think he expressed adequate gratitude for an expensive gift. Mrs. Mason exploded with rage, which surprised and distressed Hughes.[7] Only after several apologetic letters was Hughes readmitted to her favor.

Hughes ended his college experience with a bang. As part of a senior course in sociology, Hughes conducted a survey of Lincoln students. Although questions about all aspects of campus life were asked, Hughes's real purpose was to reveal opinions on the school's all-white faculty. As he expected, Hughes's findings showed that a majority of Lincoln students *did not want* black professors. This indicated to Hughes "that the college itself has failed in instilling in these students the very quality of self-reliance and self-respect which any capable American leader should have—and the purpose of this college, let us remember, is to educate 'leaders of the colored people.'"[8] The report was deliberately leaked to the African-American press. As a result of Hughes's findings,

African Americans were added to Lincoln's faculty and trustees within a few years.

Hughes graduated in June 1929. A few months later, the stock market crash plunged the country into the Great Depression. African Americans' economic gains of the 1920s were erased. The Harlem Renaissance was essentially over.

After graduation, Hughes again spent the summer at Lincoln. He revised and polished his novel, a process he found difficult. "I couldn't bear to have the people I had grown to love locked up in long pages of uncomfortable words," he said of his characters.[9]

In the country's deepening economic depression, the twenty-eight-year-old Hughes did not need to look for work. Mrs. Mason continued to support him. One day, he rode up to Pennsylvania Railroad Station in New York City in Mrs. Mason's chauffeured limousine. A dozen porters pressed forward to take his bags. They were eager for any tips they might earn. With surprise and dismay, Hughes recognized several of them. They were his former college classmates, unable to get better jobs after graduation the previous year. Yet they did not begrudge him his success. They shook his hand, slapped him on the back and congratulated him on his good fortune.[10]

The revisions to his novel were at last completed in Westfield, New Jersey. Mrs. Mason had decided he should take a room in a boardinghouse there, away

Langston Hughes, pictured in his 1929 Lincoln University yearbook. Hughes had returned to college as a published poet at age twenty-four after several years of traveling the world as a merchant seaman.

from the distractions of New York. In February 1930, Hughes gave the manuscript, called *Not Without Laughter*, to his publisher and fell into a period of inactivity. Mrs. Mason was displeased.

By spring, however, Hughes had a literary partner. She was the African-American writer and folklorist Zora Neale Hurston. Hurston was also Mrs. Mason's protégée. Mrs. Mason had hired a secretary for them to share, an African-American former teacher named Louise Thompson. Hughes and Hurston decided to work together on a comic play they called *Mule Bone*. For a while, they made good progress writing. Then Hurston abruptly departed for a trip down South, leaving the play unfinished.

No sooner had she gone than Mrs. Mason ended her relationship with Hughes. In a terrible scene, she raged at him about his ingratitude. The money she had showered on him, she asserted, had been all for nothing. Hughes was stunned.[11] It later became apparent that Hurston was jealous of the younger and prettier Louise Thompson. Hurston had falsely told Mrs. Mason that Hughes was romantically involved with their secretary. She claimed that Hughes and Thompson had left her alone to work on the play. Hurston undoubtedly wanted Thompson fired but may not have realized that Mrs. Mason would react so drastically.[12]

Although he never saw Mrs. Mason again, it took

Hughes months to accept that their break was final. He was stricken with psychosomatic illness.[13] An award of four hundred dollars by the Harmon Foundation in early 1931 for his novel came as a godsend. This award had been established a few years before to recognize African-American contributions to the fine arts.

Hughes knew he needed a change. He decided to head toward the sun. With Zell Ingram, an artist friend from Cleveland, Hughes drove south in a car borrowed from Ingram's mother. From Key West, Florida, the two men sailed to Cuba in April 1931. This was Hughes's third visit to the island. The first had been as a merchant seaman. On his second visit, traveling with Charlotte Mason's money, Hughes had met his Cuban contemporaries as a successful writer. This time, Hughes and Ingram were wined and dined by the intellectual elite of Havana. Hughes was a hero to the authors there.

It was in Haiti, where they journeyed next, that Hughes truly renewed his spirit. Haiti was the first black-ruled country in the Western Hemisphere. A great revolt there had succeeded in driving out the French slaveowners. Hughes's grandmother Mary Langston had been offered a pension and a place of honor in Haiti because of her first husband's role years earlier in John Brown's raid. On the island, Hughes stopped writing. He stopped writing and simply lived. He lay in the sun, danced, drank, and fished with the "people without shoes."[14] In this all-black atmosphere, rich with history, music, and folk art, he shook off the hurt of his manipulation by Charlotte Mason. He came home a new man in July 1931.

He had also renewed his social conscience. The economic oppression of dark people he saw so clearly in Cuba and Haiti struck him forcibly. He connected it with colonial exploitation in Africa and racist exploitation of African-American labor in the South. He was ready to reject the economic system that had plunged the United States into the Great Depression.

Still, he had to earn a living. Although he was the author of a novel and two volumes of poetry, he had made relatively little money from writing. At Lincoln University, he had fulfilled the teacher training requirements, but Hughes decided teaching was not for him. Nor would he ever again accept menial jobs or be supported by a patron. In the face of misfortune, his determination to make a living from writing—his goal since high school—hardened:

> For ten years I had been a writer of sorts, but a writer who wrote mostly because, when I felt bad, writing kept me from feeling worse. . . . Now . . . I had to make a living from writing itself. So, of necessity, I began to turn poetry into bread.[15]

Besides, he wrote, "I wanted to write seriously and

as well as I knew how about the Negro people, and make that kind of writing earn for me a living."[16]

It was Mary McLeod Bethune, the great African-American educator, who showed him the way. When Hughes had passed through Daytona Beach, Florida, on his way to the Caribbean, Mrs. Bethune welcomed him to Bethune-Cookman College with open arms. She stayed up late to talk to him. She suggested that he tour the country, sharing poetry with African-American audiences.

Now he was ready to accept Mary McLeod Bethune's challenge to bring "poetry to the people."[17] He applied for a Rosenwald Foundation grant. The family of the founders of Sears, Roebuck and Company had established a fund "to aid Negro education."[18] Hughes proposed a poetry-reading tour like none before. He would speak to audiences that had never met an African-American author, perhaps had never even heard of one. The Rosenwald Foundation awarded him one thousand dollars. With the money, Hughes bought a car and printed inexpensive editions of his poems, which he planned to sell. He also prepared a display of books by black authors from all over the world.

For several months he crisscrossed the South and West, reading at churches, schools, colleges, and community centers. Although his fee was supposed to be one hundred dollars, he would take half or a quarter of that. He even read for free if a community was too poor to pay. Nothing like this tour had ever been seen in the South. "I've never had a finer response anywhere, or met more beautiful people," he reported to the foundation. "Even in the backwoods, they seemed to know what I was talking about, and to appreciate it."[19] When he again passed through Daytona Beach, he gave a reading at Bethune-Cookman College. The climax of his performance came with the reading of his poem "The Negro Mother." Hughes looked up to see Mrs. Bethune, rising with tears in her eyes to embrace him. "My son, my son," she cried.[20]

At Christmastime, Hughes spent the break at Oakwood Junior College in Alabama. His friend Arna Bontemps had taken a teaching position there. Hughes and Bontemps decided to write a children's story together, based on Hughes's Haitian experiences. *Popo and Fifina* was published the following year. It was the first of many collaborations between the two writers over the next thirty-five years.

The tour was cut short in June 1932, when Hughes received a thrilling invitation. He was asked to be a writer for a movie to be made in Soviet Russia, the home of socialism and revolution. He hoped to see a nonexploitative economic system and a nonracist social system there. He leapt at the opportunity.

7

ACROSS RUSSIA, AROUND THE WORLD

The motion picture *Black and White*, which would be made in Russia, was intended to be the first serious film about American race relations. Twenty-two African Americans made up the film troupe. Strangely, only two of them were trained actors. Louise Thompson, Hughes's friend and former secretary, was the group's leader. Only one of the twenty-two was a member of the American branch of the Communist party.

They were hailed as celebrities when they arrived in Moscow. A few days later they were presented with contracts—in Russian. "I can't read a word of it," Hughes declared, looking at the document, "and I won't sign something I can't read."[1] After a week's delay, his employers offered him the English-language version. Hughes was happy to find an offer of four months' guaranteed work at the highest salary he had ever received. He was free to begin enjoying it immediately, too. There would be a delay of thirty days until he had to begin writing. The scenario, or story outline of the film, was not yet complete.

When at last the story outline arrived, it, too, was in Russian. More difficulties arose as the translation was being prepared. The director was a German who did not speak English or Russian and had never made a major film. The lead actor was a delicate-looking dancer. He did not seem to Hughes to be suited to the role of a brawny labor organizer.

It only got worse. The scenario translation was a socialist fantasy of race relations in the South. In it, African-American steelworkers in Birmingham, Alabama, were being organized into a union by a white labor organizer. The white factory owners tried to turn the white steelworkers against their black coworkers, leading to a race riot. At the height of the riot, wealthy African Americans supposedly broadcast on their private radio station for help. Northern white union members then came to their rescue. Hughes realized no film could be made from the absurd script.

Still, the film company wanted to proceed and ordered the scenario revised. Again the troupe was left with time on its hands. The actors plodded ahead with musical rehearsals but began to get bored and quarrelsome. Some of them, who had dreamed of being movie stars, realized their dreams might not come true. Still, they were being paid and living in luxury.

Finally, shooting was scheduled to begin on August 15, close to the end of the brief Russian summer, in the southern resort city of Odessa. When the troupe arrived, an associate was waiting for them with a copy of the Paris *Herald-Tribune* in hand. "Soviet Calls Off Film on U.S. Negroes; Fear of American Reaction Cause" read the headline.[2]

It appears that in addition to the film company's bungling, politics had played a role in the disaster that was *Black and White*. The United States, which had never recognized the legitimacy of the Soviet government after the 1917 Russian Revolution, was about to do so. Influential Americans in Moscow were angry that the film was to be critical of United States race relations. They successfully appealed to the Communists. In order to win recognition, the Soviet government ordered the film canceled.

The twenty-two would-be actors were outraged. Some felt the black race had been betrayed.[3] Finally, they accepted the inevitable. At least they would be paid in full for four months' work, even though less than two months had passed. They were offered full-paid tours of the country, or tickets home, either direct or via Europe. Hughes decided to accept the tour.

As a writer, Hughes was faring better than the others in the Soviet Union. He was receiving sizable cash advances from Soviet publishers. His novel *Not Without Laughter* and volumes of his poetry were to be translated and published. At home, too, he was meeting with critical success. His first two children's books, *The Dream Keeper*, a selection of his poems for young people, and *Popo and Fifina* both met with high praise from critics.

Along with ten former members of the film troupe, Hughes began a tour of Uzbekistan, Kazakhstan, and Turkmenistan, in the Soviet Far East. It took five days to travel from Moscow to Asia, across the desolate Soviet grasslands. On the train, Hughes saw the first evidence that what he had heard about the elimination of racism was true. He and his friends met a simply dressed traveler in his twenties from Uzbekistan. Probably a factory worker, Hughes thought. To his amazement, he found that the young man was the mayor of the ancient city of Bokhara, where they were headed. The Uzbek's skin was the color of Hughes's own. "In the Soviet Union dark men are also the mayors of cities," Hughes noted with pleasure.[4]

For almost two weeks, the Americans toured the republic of Uzbekistan as guests of the Soviet Union.

Arna Bontemps was Langston Hughes's best friend for more than forty years. The two writers wrote many books together, beginning with *Popo and Fifina* in 1931.

They followed a busy schedule of visits to farms, factories, and schools, accompanied by banquets and speeches. The short visit made a deep impression. Everywhere, they saw evidence of the progress being made by these formerly very primitive societies and their dark-skinned peoples. They saw dark-skinned people running literacy and health programs. They saw Jews and other minority ethnic groups, previously denied many rights, participating in civic life. They saw women freed from veils, harems, and marriage-by-purchase. They saw African-American engineers and agricultural chemists treated as valued professionals by their Soviet employers. "The past ten days have been the greatest of my whole life," Louise Thompson wrote to her mother.[5] Still, the hectic pace of the tour exhausted the Americans. All but Hughes voted to return to Moscow.

Hughes, a great traveler, had always particularly hated segregated public transportation in the United States. In the Uzbek city of Tashkent, he noticed partitions in the middle of the streetcars, separating the seats into two sections. He asked an Uzbek friend what the partition was for. Before the Revolution, he was told, it had separated the Europeans from the Asians. In other words, Hughes thought, the white people from the colored people.[6] Now this segregation had ended.

Many people wondered during the 1930s how a

man who valued personal freedom as much as Langston Hughes did could admire the Soviet Union so much. As the years went by and Soviet cruelties became more well known, he did lose much of his admiration. However, he always viewed the Soviets' outlawing of racial discrimination as their greatest accomplishment. Before legal segregation ended in the United States, he wrote, "White Americans say it will take a hundred years, or two or three generations, to wipe out segregation in the South. But in Tashkent it had taken only a few years—and a willingness on the part of the government to enforce decent racial laws."[7]

The three months Hughes spent traveling on his own confirmed his judgment. He visited the fabled and beautiful Muslim cities of the region. He met the common people, eating and drinking with them from a single container of stew or tea. He made hundreds of friends, from journalists to camel drivers.

In January 1933, he returned to Moscow for six months. Two things kept him abroad. In the deepening Great Depression he would have found it hard to support himself in the United States. Despite critical praise, his five published books were earning him only a trickle of royalty payments. In the Soviet Union he was making a good living from his books and the articles he wrote for the English-language Soviet press.

The greater attraction, however, was a new love— one that would bring him as close to marriage as he would ever get. Sylvia Chen was a professional dancer, half Chinese and half Afro-Caribbean and French. Her father, a Chinese socialist, had settled the family temporarily in the Soviet Union. She and Hughes had met during the film-making fiasco. When they became reacquainted on his return to Moscow, they fell in love. Sylvia Chen would remember him as "charming . . . jolly . . . and so natural." She had great "admiration for his integrity and art."[8] He, in turn, described her as "a delicate, flowerlike girl, beautiful in a reedy, golden-skinned sort of way."[9]

The two spent much time together that winter and thought of marriage. Again, as with Anne-Marie Coussey, Hughes was unwilling to make a commitment. When Chen left Moscow to tour with her program of dances, he let the relationship cool. They continued to write, but had no plans to meet again.

Hughes traveled by the Trans-Siberian Railway to begin his return to the United States. After leaving the Soviet Union, Hughes visited Korea, China, Japan, and Hawaii. He had been on the road for over a year. Hughes arrived in San Francisco by ship on August 9, 1933. He was returning to a country in crisis. Unemployment and business failures were reaching record levels. His ability to live by writing would be sorely tested.

8

LET AMERICA BE
AMERICA AGAIN

irst of all, Hughes needed to find a place to live. The wealthy San Francisco bachelor Noel Sullivan took care of that. The two men had met during one of Hughes's poetry reading tours. Sullivan liked to use his great inherited wealth for the benefit of the arts and liberal causes. Unlike Charlotte Mason, he did not attach strings to his gifts.

Sullivan offered Hughes the use of his vacation home in Carmel, California, on Monterey Bay. The peaceful seaside community was the perfect spot for Hughes to write without interruption. He also socialized with the many well-known artists and writers there in the early 1930s.

Hughes immediately began to write a travel book about his experiences in Central Asia. He also assembled his radical, Soviet-inspired poems for publication. Both volumes were promptly rejected by Knopf, his publisher. Knopf considered them propaganda and artistically unworthy of him. "Good Morning, Revolution," one of the best-known of these, reads

> *Good-morning, Revolution:*
> *You're the very best friend*
> *I ever had.*
> *We gonna pal around together from now on.*[1]

Hughes had better luck with short fiction. While still in Moscow, he was inspired by a book of short stories by D. H. Lawrence. A great stream of his own stories resulted. In 1934, they were collected and published to critical acclaim in *The Ways of White Folks*.

Hughes began to think once more about Sylvia Chen. Impulsively, after seven months' silence, he wrote to her on January 1, 1934. "Come on over this way, will you?" he asked. A hurt Chen answered, "I suppose one of your New Year duties is to write to all your girl 'friends' who are scattered over the world, and tell them you remember them."[2] Several more half-teasing, half-serious letters went back and forth. Then in July, Hughes wrote, "I want you, Sylvia baby, more than anyone else in the world, believe it or not. I love you."[3]

He was serious, at least for a while. He even consulted a lawyer about the law of immigration and marriage, but he made no proposal to her. By fall, she could wait no longer. She married another American suitor, the film critic Jay Leyda. A few years later, she and Hughes would meet in New York. He would blurt out his regret: "Why did you do it? How could you give up what we had and marry someone else?"[4] It was his last serious attachment to a woman.

Although Hughes wrote a great deal in Carmel, it was with mixed results financially and artistically. During his year there, Hughes was also more deeply involved in radical activity than at any other time. He participated in rallies and fund-raising, and wrote about labor and socialist issues. His actions caught the attention of conservative forces in northern California. He was attacked in writing by the Carmel newspaper. Told that he would be the target of violence by the Vigilantes, a white supremacist group, Hughes fled by night to Reno, Nevada.

There, he settled into an African-American boardinghouse to write. Unexpectedly, he received news of his father's death in October 1934. Hughes doubted that he would inherit anything, even when he received a telegram telling him to come to Mexico for the settlement of his father's estate. Sure enough, after borrowing money to make the journey, Hughes found out that he had been left nothing. James Hughes's business partners were three Mexican ladies, who remembered Langston fondly from his adolescence. They insisted on sharing at least part of the legacy with him.

This time, Hughes loved Mexico. He spent almost eight months there, living a carefree existence full of parties, nightclubs, bullfights, and literary gatherings. He moved among Mexico's most renowned artists and writers as an equal. He returned to America in mid-1935, having been awarded a grant for his writing. He paid his debts with the inheritance and merely came out even.

In September 1935, Hughes arrived in New York for his first visit in more than three years. To his amazement, he found out that his play *Mulatto*, adapted from one of the stories in *The Ways of White Folks*,[5] was about to open on Broadway. It seems that his theatrical agent had neglected to notify him. Hughes signed the necessary contracts that day.

Hughes hurried to the theater, where he scarcely recognized the play being rehearsed. The white producer Martin Jones had completely rewritten it, making it much more sensational and violent. That was not all. Jones now refused to pay the five hundred dollars due to Hughes. He planned to segregate theater seating by race. Then he did not invite the

African-American cast members or Hughes to the opening night party. When Hughes protested, his agent asked whether he wanted a hit or not. Hughes gave in. The reviews praised the actors, but the critics were scathing toward its supposed author, calling the play "weary," "shrill," "vulgar," and "merely a bad play."[6]

Still, Hughes had his hit. *Mulatto* had the longest Broadway run of any play by an African-American author until the 1950s. Several touring companies produced it throughout the country. Thanks to negotiation by the Dramatists Guild, Jones did give Hughes his five hundred dollars. Every other payment during the show's long Broadway run had to be pried out of the producer, though. Hughes never received the full amount due.

When some money finally began to come in, Hughes had a new and serious use for it. His mother was dying of cancer. While he was still in Mexico, Carrie Clark had discovered a lump in her breast. She had been too frightened to see a doctor. Just before *Mulatto* opened, she had finally been diagnosed. She was advised to have surgery at once, but refused.

As difficult as their relationship had been over the years, Hughes was moved by her illness.[7] When she took a turn for the worse, he wired his stepbrother: "SEND MAMA ANY HOSPITAL NECESSARY

REGARDLESS COST."[8] Against all expectation, Carrie Clark lived nearly three more years. She received the best care at her son's expense. Her illness left him, once again, financially drained. Ironically, many of his friends and associates believed that he was wealthy because of the success of his play.

In the spring of 1937, Hughes received an invitation to represent the United States at an International Writers Congress. From there, he proceeded to war-torn Spain as a journalist to cover its civil war for several newspapers. On his trip, Hughes met several black writers from French colonies in Africa and the Caribbean. They looked up to him as the world's premier author of African descent.

The conflict in Spain was seen by many as a precursor of World War II (1939–1945). In Spain, fascist forces led by Generalissimo Francisco Franco were trying to overthrow the legally elected liberal government. On Franco's side were the army, the rich, and the church. He had imported troops from Spanish colonies in Africa. He was supplied with men and arms by his fellow fascists, Benito Mussolini of Italy and Adolf Hitler of Germany. On the government's side were the common people. Freedom-loving young people from all over the world had come to fight on the government's, or Loyalists', side. They were known as the International Brigades. Arms for the government forces came partly from the Soviet Union. Although they put up a valiant fight, the Loyalists would lose in only two more years.

Hughes was particularly interested in writing about the several hundred black soldiers of the International Brigades. They had left their homes in the United States, the Caribbean, Africa, and elsewhere to fight voluntarily on the Loyalist side. He was also interested in contrasting them to the drafted African troops on the fascist side. Hughes stayed more than six months in Spain, longer than he had intended. He sent back numerous dispatches and again wrote much poetry. One powerful poem, "Today," reads:

> *This is earthquake*
> *Weather!*
> *Honor and hunger*
> *Walk lean*
> *Together.*[9]

He grew to love Spain and its valiant people very much.[10] He saw the parallel between African Americans struggling for freedom in the United States and Spaniards struggling for freedom in Spain. He wrote:

> In the last few years, I had been all around the embattled world and I had seen people walking tightropes everywhere—the tightrope of color in Alabama . . . of war itself in . . . Spain—and myself everywhere on my tightrope of words.[11]

In January 1938, after returning from Spain, Hughes spoke to a group in Paris about conditions during the Spanish Civil War.

Hughes would have liked to stay with the International Brigades, but he knew that food supplies for the soldiers and civilians were limited. They did not need another mouth to feed. It was time for him to go back to the United States.

Inspired by the traveling people's theaters of Spain, Hughes returned to New York in January 1938 eager to create his own drama group. He would call it the Suitcase Theater. Hughes wanted to show that theater could be produced with merely the contents of a suitcase. Like the experimental theaters of the Soviet Union, Hughes's play would have the action extend into and around the audience.

With a group of amateur actors, Hughes opened his first play in mid-1938. It was a production of dramatic scenes, his own poetry, and traditional African-American music. *Don't You Want to Be Free?* was a smash hit. It would be performed on and off for three years, the longest run of any play in Harlem, where it remained. The lead was played by Robert Earl Jones, father of the actor James Earl Jones, in his first starring role.

Now that both of his parents were dead, Hughes was free to write about his young life. In late 1939, he retreated to Noel Sullivan's new farm, near Carmel, to write his autobiography. *The Big Sea* was published the following year to much praise but few sales.

Robert Earl Jones, father of the actor James Earl Jones, had his first starring role in Hughes's play *Don't You Want to Be Free?* The show was a smash hit.

The 1930s had been a decade full of drastic ups and downs for Hughes. Artistically, he had gone from triumph to embarrassment; financially, from comparative affluence to near poverty; personally, from exhilaration to sadness. This pattern would continue in the 1940s.

9

I DREAM A
WORLD

Hughes was disappointed at the slight success of *The Big Sea* when it was published in 1940. This was made worse by an unexpected attack on him by religious and political conservatives. A popular radio evangelist picketed the hotel where Hughes was to speak about his autobiography. Her stated reason was a poem called "Goodbye, Christ," which he had written in the Soviet Union. It had been published in a black socialist magazine in Europe without his permission. The popular weekly *Saturday Evening Post* magazine continued to attack him in print. At the end of the year, Hughes decided to issue a formal repudiation of the poem, saying that it no longer represented his beliefs. This did not stop the harassment, however. It continued for almost fifteen years.

The involvement of the United States in World War II provided him with the opportunity to demonstrate his patriotism. He also continued to serve, even more forcefully than before, as a spokesman for his race. Hughes never missed an opportunity to point out that Hitler hated blacks as much as he hated Jews. Hughes did not think the Japanese were any better, even though they were also non-white. He had been harassed by the Japanese police and expelled from the country on a brief stopover there in 1933. He believed the Japanese empire was just as racist as the Nazis.

Hughes realized that World War II would bring many changes, including an end to segregation at home and colonialism in the third world. He knew that the United States could not pretend to defend democracy abroad while denying it to African Americans at home. Nor could it even win the war without the African-American effort in defense industries and the armed forces. There, segregation was being slowly, but surely, challenged. Furthermore, he foresaw that the dark people of colonized countries would soon demand their freedom, too.

Hughes was asked to serve on the Writers' War

Board. He turned out songs, patriotic slogans, jingles, and radio scripts promoting the war effort. In these, he never hesitated to praise African-American accomplishments in war and to demand equal treatment. Some of his writings were turned down as too forceful. Hughes condemned this censorship.

Hughes was briefly eligible to be drafted into the army. He considered enlisting to obtain a journalistic, rather than a combat, assignment. Hughes made this forthright statement to his draft board: "I wish to register herewith, as a citizen of the United States, my complete disapproval of the segregating of the armed forces of the United States into White and Negro units."[1] Then President Franklin Delano Roosevelt deferred the draft for men over thirty-eight. Hughes, at forty-one, was no longer in danger of being called to service.

Sometimes Hughes was paid a small amount for his war work. Much of it was done as a volunteer. The early 1940s were perhaps Hughes's leanest years in terms of income. His bank balance frequently fell into the one-to-two-dollar range. He had no savings. At one point, he could not attend dinner parties requiring a coat and tie because he had pawned his last remaining suit. At another point, he had to ask his friend Arna Bontemps for a loan to buy toothpaste and shaving cream.

Hughes was also essentially homeless during the

This portrait of Langston Hughes was taken by the great African-American photojournalist and writer Gordon Parks in 1943. Both Parks, who was working for the United States Office of War Information, and Hughes did much to support their country in World War II.

early 1940s. He was evicted from his Harlem apartment in 1940. His stepbrother, Gwyn Clark, who was living there while Hughes was in California, had not paid the rent. When not traveling as part of his poetry-reading tours or war work, Hughes lived with friends for long periods of time. He also became the first African American to be invited to stay at Yaddo, outside Saratoga, New York. Yaddo, a unique retreat for writers, musicians, and artists, hosted Hughes in the summers of 1941 and 1942.

In 1941, Knopf published *Shakespeare in Harlem*, its first full volume since 1926 of adult poetry by Hughes. "Merry-Go-Round," from this book, became one of his most frequently quoted poems.

> *Down South on the train*
> *There's a Jim Crow car.*
> *On the bus we're put in the back—*
> *But there ain't no back*
> *To a merry-go-round!*
> *Where's the horse*
> *For a kid that's black.*[2]

His relationship with his publisher had become strained. Knopf had repeatedly rejected his radical poetry during the 1930s. None of his six previous books had sold well. The company considered him a minor poetic talent. Knopf offered him a flat fee in place of further royalty payments on all his books before *The Big Sea*. Hughes, who was financially desperate, resentfully agreed. Three years later, after saving enough money, the first thing Hughes did was to negotiate the return of his royalty payments.

Hughes's greatest artistic achievement of the early 1940s came about almost by accident. The Chicago *Defender*, the country's most prominent African-American newspaper, offered him a weekly column in 1941. For a while, in "Here to Yonder," he offered opinions on a variety of topics. Then in 1943, Hughes began to write the column in the form of a barstool conversation. It featured an educated, slightly pompous narrator and his "simple-minded friend." This naive—but highly accurate and humorous—observer of the political and racial scene came to be known as Jesse B. Semple, or "Simple."

The Simple columns were an immediate sensation in the African-American community. Reams of mail addressed to Simple were sent to Hughes, along with cakes and other gifts. Soldiers Hughes met during the war always wanted to know how Simple was doing. The columns were eventually acknowledged by critics to be superb journalism in the highest tradition of Mark Twain and other humorists.

Hughes's war work had made him known to whites as one of the most prominent spokesmen on racial issues. A 1944 radio broadcast called "Let's Face the Race Question" was a personal triumph. In it Hughes and a white liberal debated two segregationists. This brought him to the attention of one of the country's leading lecture bureaus, the Feakins Agency. Under its sponsorship, Hughes went on a lucrative lecture tour, appearing before mostly white audiences. As the war ended in 1945, Hughes was finally back on his feet financially and eager for the opportunities of peacetime.

An unprecedented opportunity presented itself. The Pulitzer Prize–winning dramatist Elmer Rice was adapting his play *Street Scene* as an opera. The distinguished German-Jewish composer Kurt Weill was providing the music. They asked Hughes to be their lyricist, writing the words to the songs. Rice and Weill hoped to bring the show to Broadway. Blacks had contributed to all-black musicals in the past. Still, never before had an African American, with white collaborators, provided all the song lyrics for a musical show featuring a white cast.

The choice of Langston Hughes by Rice and Weill was unexpected, but it made sense. *Street Scene* was to chronicle the life-and-death dramas of the poor, multiethnic tenants of a city apartment building. "They wanted someone who understood the problems of the common people," Hughes said. Weill added that they wanted a writer who could "lift the everyday language of the people into a simple, unsophisticated poetry."[3] Hughes was perfect.

Street Scene played on Broadway for four months in 1947. Hughes earned several thousand dollars a week during its run, the most he would ever make. He proudly asked Carl Van Vechten for investment advice, but he had a plan for his newfound wealth. He would buy his own home.

Along with his friends Toy and Emerson Harper, Hughes bought a handsome, historic, three-story brownstone at 20 East 127th Street, in the heart of Harlem. Hughes had lived with the Harpers, on and off, since 1935. Ethel Harper was called "Toy" because of her petite size. She was a well-known Harlem dressmaker and a childhood friend of Carrie Clark. Her husband, Emerson, was an accomplished professional musician.

Hughes's relationship with the Harpers was unique. He called them "Aunt Toy" and "Uncle Emerson." The childless couple, in their turn, truly loved him like a son. At the age of forty-six, Hughes had at last found a completely happy family.

They intended to make the large dwelling pay for itself as a boardinghouse. Like Simple, Hughes lived in the "third floor rear," overlooking the garden. The two-room office/bedroom suite suited him completely. A visitor described the studio as filled with "many hundreds of books, African curios, and record albums [vying] for space with manuscripts, letters, clippings, plaques and filing cases."[4] The Harpers lived on the

Langston Hughes watches the Skyloft Players of Chicago rehearse his play *The Sun Do Move* in April 1942. Hughes's greatest success in drama came with the musical *Street Scene* in the 1950s.

first floor. Hughes often ate with them between travels and social engagements.

Hughes would not enjoy this prosperity and prominence for long, however. The anti-Communist movement began to harass him again. J. Edgar Hoover, the fanatically anti-Communist director of the FBI, submitted a speech (read by an underling) to a convention of Methodist ministers. The speech was broadcast on radio and printed in newspapers.

The speech contained a number of ridiculously untrue charges. It accused Hughes of being a Communist party member (he never had been), and also of running for office on the Communist party ticket (he had not). In addition, it claimed that he had married a white woman and identified her by name. He had never even met the woman.

The speech put Hughes, who was in the midst of a well-paying cross-country lecture tour, on the defensive. It seems as if it should have been easy to clear his name, but it was not. The press kept repeating the accusations without verifying them. The word of a powerful man like Hoover was enough to keep them circulating. The Feakins lecture agency dropped Hughes as a client. He went back to speaking primarily to African-American audiences in schools, churches, and colleges. Hughes noted ironically that anti-Communists seemed to leave him alone when he kept to his own race.

In the late 1940s Hughes tried teaching for the first time. In the winter semester of 1947, Hughes taught creative writing and "The Negro in American Poetry" at the historically black Atlanta University. A student described him as "shy and . . . painfully reticent in responding to personal questions."[5] She believed years later that his course laid the foundation for future African-American studies programs. It was the first at that college to be taught from a black perspective.

Two years later, Hughes tried a more varied and challenging teaching job. The Laboratory School of the University of Chicago was an experimental, racially integrated school for children from age four through high school. Hughes was hired as Visiting Lecturer on Poetry for three months. He did everything from helping kindergartners write stories, to teaching about Mexico for a geography class, to lecturing on autobiography and jazz.

Hughes loved children and they responded strongly to him as a teacher. He believed they were more receptive to poetry than were adults. "Some of my kids are turning in some BEAUTIFUL creative work," he wrote to Arna Bontemps. "Better, I regret to say, than my Southern college kids did, freer and more original stuff."[6] Although he enjoyed both of these teaching experiences, Hughes preferred the freedom of writing and lecturing to the fixed schedule of the classroom. He did not teach again.

Hughes had two volumes of poetry published by Knopf after the war: *Fields of Wonder* in 1947 and *One Way Ticket* in 1949. He continued to celebrate the theme of African-American (and his own) survival in his poems. In "Life Is Fine," he wrote:

> *Though you may hear me holler,*
> *And you may see me cry—*
> *I'll be dogged, sweet baby,*
> *If you gonna see me die.*[7]

In 1948, he wrote furiously for a week, inspired by jazz's newest development, known as bebop. He composed a suite of poems called "Montage of a Dream Deferred." It was published as a book in 1951. In such famous poems as "Harlem," this collection showed that his power was undiminished. The poem begins:

> *What happens to a dream deferred?*
>
> > *Does it dry up*
> > *like a raisin in the sun?*
> > *Or fester like a sore—*
> > *And then run?*[8]

For his greatest commercial successes of the late 1940s he sought other publishers. Knopf was later embarrassed to have turned both projects down. *The Poetry of the Negro* was a landmark anthology compiled by Hughes and Bontemps. For years to come, it was considered by critics to be the best collection of its kind. With *Simple Speaks His Mind*, Hughes had his most highly praised book yet. It sold thirty thousand copies, more than all his poetry books combined.

As the 1940s ended, Hughes could feel satisfaction at having found a home and family. He had broken new ground artistically with the creation of Simple. He never wavered from his goal of making a living by writing. The anti-Communist movement was not through with him yet, however. There were difficult times ahead of him still. In the 1950s, his fortunes would reach their lowest ebb. He would struggle to be heard and at times would barely make a living, but he would endure and finally prosper.

10

WITCH HUNT

ughes's artistic output reached its all-time low in the early 1950s. He published good, even excellent, journalism and children's books but wasted much of his time on unsuccessful musical and literary collaborations. Again, his financial situation was desperate. At Christmastime 1952, his bank balance stood at $9.04.[1] By this time, he no longer wrote only when unhappy. He had become the ultimate writing professional. He wrote constantly, sometimes eighteen hours a day. Only that and continual speaking tours put food on his table and paid his mortgage. He and a succession of secretaries juggled his various writing projects by using color-coded paper for each one.

In 1953, the anti-Communist movement's persecution of Hughes reached a climax and played itself out. He was forced to testify before the United States Senate's Permanent Sub-Committee on Investigations. Its leader was Senator Joseph McCarthy of Wisconsin. The committee believed that Hughes, whose books were included in State Department libraries abroad, was aiding Communism with his writings.

During the Cold War after World War II, the United States considered the Soviet Union and other Communist countries to be its greatest enemies. Americans who were thought to agree with Communist beliefs were considered enemies as well. McCarthy was an ardent anti-Communist who led a series of "witch hunts" during the early 1950s. These were intended to identify and destroy the lives of people who were, had been, or were suspected of being members of the Communist party of the United States. Though membership was perfectly legal, these people, after being "named," would often lose their jobs and be shunned in their communities. Many people who had never even belonged to the party were pulled into this dragnet.

On March 26, Hughes, supported by an NAACP lawyer, testified at a televised hearing. His testimony outlined his beliefs and how they changed. His interest in the Soviet economic and political system grew, he stated, during the 1930s, as a result of the Great Depression and his visit to the Soviet Union. By 1950, it had declined. First, the Nazi-Soviet pact, by which Hitler and Stalin formed a short-lived alliance before World War II, had been a shock. Then, following the war, the Soviet Union's takeover of Eastern Europe and word of official Soviet anti-Semitism had disillusioned him. All along, he said, he had disapproved of the Soviet lack of freedom of speech and expression.[2]

Though he did not say so to McCarthy's committee, his strongest reason for separating himself from the supporters of the Soviet system was their overwhelming whiteness. He continued to agree with many of their social, economic, and political goals. Still, he realized that these goals would never be accepted by the African-American masses. This was partly because of black suspicion of being manipulated by whites. It was also because Communist atheism was unthinkable to the deeply spiritual African-American community. In the end, the esteem of the black world was far more important to Hughes than that of his white comrades.[3]

The committee asked him only a few questions, which he answered truthfully. Once he was dismissed by McCarthy, Hughes's persecution by anti-Communists was largely over. Certain charges

After years of harassment by the anti-Communist movement, Langston Hughes was called to testify before the United States Senate's Permanent Sub-Committee on Investigations in March 1953. This committee was chaired by Senator Joseph McCarthy of Wisconsin.

would continue to arise, even as late as the 1960s, but they would never significantly interfere with his life again.

Ironically, this exposure led to renewed interest in the second volume of his autobiography, which was about his experiences in Russia. Hughes again took up the story of his globe-circling travels during the 1930s, which he had been writing on and off since his return. *I Wonder As I Wander* was published by Rinehart and Company in 1956.

During the early 1950s, Hughes took fewer trips for pleasure than at any other time in his well-traveled life. He was working long hours to support himself but was also content to remain in his beloved Harlem. He was the only major African-American writer, he noted proudly, to keep living in the black community after achieving success. "I was in love with Harlem long before I got there, and I am still in love with it," he said.[4] Hughes loved to stroll the Harlem streets, his devoted secretary George Houston Bass reported, commenting on the passing scene with humor: "Whenever we walked, Mr. Hughes would tell me about the landmarks, the institutions, businesses, people, and the various Harlem life styles that were all very dear to him."[5]

Hughes was a well-known and well-liked figure in the neighborhood. He was particularly generous to children. He planned and organized a community garden for youngsters in front of his house. Children loved to run errands for him because he was known to be the biggest tipper on the block.

The Harlem everyman Jesse B. Semple continued his wicked commentaries on the contemporary scene during the decade, as well. Both in the *Defender* and in several books, Semple had his say, particularly about the strengthening civil rights movement. A successful musical, *Simply Heavenly*, based by Hughes on his characters from the Simple columns, played in New York for several months.

Hughes avidly followed the successes of the civil rights movement. His Lincoln University classmate Thurgood Marshall was the winning NAACP attorney in the historic *Brown* v. *Board of Education of Topeka* Supreme Court case in 1954. The Court's ruling overturned legal support of segregated schools. Interestingly, it was in this same city that Carrie Hughes had won the right to send young Langston to an all-white first grade.

With his loathing of segregated transportation, Hughes particularly followed accounts of the victory of the Montgomery Bus Boycott. The December 1955 boycott had begun when a black woman named Rosa Parks refused to give up her seat in the "white" section of a segregated city bus. Hughes met the hero of Montgomery, the Reverend Martin Luther King, Jr., several times. He was later asked to ghostwrite King's autobiography but declined. When King's actions generated controversy in coming years, Hughes would never tolerate criticism of him. "Me, no!" he wrote to Bontemps, "I love him."[6]

A few years later, Hughes took the opportunity to speak out before the press on the issue of segregation. Sit-in demonstrations to desegregate public facilities were sweeping the South. On a poetry-reading tour, Hughes had seen the courage of the southern students leading the protests. "Those college kids down there are TREMENDOUS!" he observed in a letter, "And not being afraid, they are beginning to win."[7]

Interest in the civil rights movement generated the first surge in black publications since the Harlem Renaissance. Publishers began to come to Hughes, soliciting his work. He and Bontemps edited the massive *Book of Negro Folklore*. Then he and author Milton Meltzer produced the landmark *Pictorial History of the Negro in America*.

Much research was required for these compilations. Hughes dug into African-American history with enthusiasm. "He prided himself on doing so much research," reported Jean Blackwell Hutson, a longtime friend who was the head of New York Public Library's Schomburg Center for Research in Black Culture. She added humorously that since he wrote at night, he would sometimes call her up during the wee hours to verify a point. Then he would be annoyed when she did not have the center's resources at hand.[8]

Publisher George Braziller obtained permission to publish the *Langston Hughes Reader*, which included poetry, stories, and essays. At last, Knopf brought out his *Selected Poems*. The stage was now set for Hughes to receive long-overdue recognition, as the full scope of his achievements began to be seen. The black community, of course, had always esteemed him. As the 1960s dawned, the white literary and cultural establishments would finally give him the honor he deserved.

11

A MODEL FOR THE WORLD

n July 1960, in a burst of poetic creativity, Hughes began to write his longest poem. "Ask Your Mama" was influenced by jazz and the African-American oral tradition, particularly the ritual insult game known as "the dozens" or "snapping."

THEY RUNG MY BELL TO ASK ME
COULD I RECOMMEND A MAID.
I SAID, YES, YOUR MAMA.[1]

It was also a sly parody of academic white poetry, with mock footnotes. Read with jazz playing in the background, it was riotously successful with black audiences. It was misunderstood and underestimated by white reviewers, however, when published as a book by Knopf in 1961.

A year after he received the Spingarn Medal, another great honor was given to Langston Hughes. In 1961 he became the second African American to be inducted into the National Institute of Arts and Letters. (The first was W.E.B. Du Bois.) This select group, limited to 250 lifetime members, represents the most highly accomplished Americans in the fields of literature and the fine arts. Hughes was inducted in the same year as his friend of forty years, Carl Van Vechten. "I see you and I are to represent the Race," he joked to Van Vechten.[2] Hughes was saluting his friend's long-time interest in black culture, as well as making a dig at the institute's nearly all-white makeup.

An unexpected pleasure was an invitation to lunch at the White House in November 1961. The occasion was a small gathering in honor of President Leopold Sedar Senghor of Senegal. The African president, a poet himself, had corresponded with Hughes for a number of years. Senghor, in his after-luncheon speech, praised Hughes as an inspiration. When he did, the American President, John F. Kennedy, looked around curiously to see who Senghor was describing. Hughes had been in disgrace with the United States government only ten years before, during the McCarthy hearings. Now

By the late 1950s, Langston Hughes was receiving long overdue recognition and honors. This portrait was taken by the United States Information Agency for overseas publicity about famous African Americans.

it was an ironic sign of progress that he was a White House guest, even if his host did not know who he was.

Hughes's most innovative work of the late 1950s and the 1960s, in addition to his continuing jazz poetry, was a series of gospel plays. Hughes pioneered this form. It combines religious themes and stories of African-American folk life with gospel music. Gospel was a unique musical form. Like jazz and the blues, it originated in the black community. Hughes's theatrical producers remained slow and uncooperative about paying author's royalties. Still, the income from the gospel plays, especially the highly successful *Black Nativity*, made the decade one of the more financially comfortable periods of his life. Hughes was able to be more selective about poetry readings and writing assignments. He was happy to indulge his great love of travel again.

Three European trips, including a cruise of the Mediterranean, gave Hughes great pleasure. Paris, with its growing multiethnic sophistication, was a particular delight. So much did he love Paris that friends believe he may have been planning to move there.

The deterioration of Harlem, with its increasing crime and drug addiction, was a source of great pain. "The teenagers of Harlem are my teenagers," he anguished in a 1963 newspaper column. "How can decent men anywhere not care about kids, black or white, who can buy marijuana and heroin without trouble almost any time?"[3] "Slum exterior in a slum district" is how a black South African journalist described Hughes's cherished Harlem home and block.[4]

Hughes's most significant and exciting travels were the four trips he made to the newly independent countries of Africa. His final trip, in 1966, was the occasion he considered one of his life's greatest honors. President Lyndon Johnson had appointed Hughes the leader of the official American delegation to the First World Festival of Negro Arts in Dakar, Senegal. There, fellow poet President Senghor again praised Hughes and recited his poetry. After Hughes's death, Senghor would say: "He will always be a model not only for the United States but for the world."[5]

Many friends and observers of Langston Hughes made note of the loneliness they saw behind his outgoing, laughing exterior.[6] Though he had hundreds of friends, Hughes had never married, had children, or even had a lengthy love affair. His close relationship with the Harpers, though, formed a sort of family. He kept up with many Hughes and Langston relatives. His relationship with his stepbrother, Gwyn Clark, an abusive alcoholic, was difficult.[7] Hughes remained fond of Clark's children, though, and remembered them in his will.

It was in friendships with young people that Hughes found some satisfaction as he grew older. He

One of the greatest honors of Langston Hughes's life was his appointment by President Lyndon Johnson as official American representative to the First World Festival of Negro Arts in Dakar, Senegal, in April 1966.

befriended and encouraged dozens of creative artists, as well as near-delinquents from his neighborhood. One of them Hughes described as having "home problems. He claims nobody likes him. I used to feel that way myself, so I understand."[8]

"He was a very caring man," said a young singer who appeared in one of Hughes's plays and became a close friend. "He was a teacher and a father and a guide."[9] Hughes's secretary George Houston Bass agreed: "I lived in the Hughes household as a member of the family—sharing the responsibilities and the privileges of home life with [the Harpers] and enjoying a father-son relationship with Langston Hughes."[10] "[He] made choices that denied him a family. But in order to compensate for that, he claimed the whole black race as his family," said Bass.[11]

As much African-American writing grew more angry, some writers accused Hughes of not being militant enough. This was partly because he used humor, rather than bitterness, to make his points. When he put Simple to rest after twenty-three years, Hughes noted sadly, "The racial climate has gotten so complicated and bitter that cheerful and ironic humor is less and less understandable to many people."[12] Yet Hughes could show his anger privately. He exploded with table-pounding force when criticized for not responding to a racial insult, Bass reported.[13]

Some of this criticism was merely ignorant, however. To Hughes the phrase "black pride" was not just a slogan but had been his way of life for forty years. "He believed in the beauty of blackness when belief in the beauty of blackness was not . . . the sweet berry of the community tooth," wrote fellow poet Gwendolyn Brooks.[14]

Deeply knowledgeable about African-American history, his pride was based on what he knew about African-American contributions to the building of America. African-American popular culture and music were admired and imitated around the globe, he had pointed out in his Spingarn Medal acceptance speech. He believed with enormous pride in African-American cultural richness and beauty.

In keeping with the times, Hughes suggested that Knopf publish a volume of his most racially militant poems. Some were recent, some dated back to the 1920s. In his sixties, he was still capable of noting ironically, "I know I am / The Negro Problem / Being wined and dined" in "Dinner Guest: Me."[15] *The Panther and the Lash* collection would be published after his death.

In May 1967, Hughes was admitted to a New York City hospital with severe abdominal pain, after several weeks of digestive problems. Not wishing any publicity and having no health insurance, he registered under the name of "James Hughes." Doctors diagnosed a

With his gift for friendship, Langston Hughes sent out hundreds of Christmas cards, starting months in advance. He hired neighborhood children to help him. This humorous card was sent in 1965.

benign mass on his enlarged prostate gland, as well as infection and heart disease. Surgery to remove his prostate was performed but did not save him. Severe infection and congestive heart failure developed. By this time, Bass had arranged for round-the-clock nursing, but it was too late. Langston Hughes died on May 22, 1967.

Hughes had designed his own funeral years before. He wished it to be a jazz and blues funeral, consisting of the African-American music he loved and celebrated. After some music, Arna Bontemps gave a brief eulogy and read several Hughes poems. Then the music began again. A jazz trio played a blues arrangement composed especially for the occasion. The funeral ended with a song specifically chosen by Hughes, with typical sly humor, as the closing number. It was Duke Ellington's "Do Nothing Till You Hear From Me." Later that day, Hughes's body was cremated as a few close friends joined hands and recited "The Negro Speaks of Rivers."

After twenty-four years, his ashes were entombed in the lobby of the Langston Hughes Auditorium at the New York Public Library's Schomberg Center for Research in Black Culture. The day would have been his eighty-ninth birthday. A mosaic design, called "Rivers," is embedded in the floor to mark his burial place. On that day, the country's most prominent

African-American creative artists danced and partied on his grave. They called it an "ancient rite of ancestral return," a celebration of Langston Hughes's life and accomplishments.[16] The partygoers wore red, as he requested in his poem "Wake." Langston Hughes would have loved it.

CHRONOLOGY

1902—James Langston Hughes born February 1 in Joplin, Missouri.

1903—Parents separate; father moves to Mexico.

1909—Goes to live with grandmother in Lawrence, Kansas.

1915—Death of grandmother, Mary Langston.

1916—Graduates from eighth grade in Lincoln, Illinois.

1919—Reunites with father in Mexico for summer.

1920—Graduates from Central High School, Cleveland, Ohio.

1921—First poem for adults, "The Negro Speaks of Rivers," published; begins college at Columbia University.

1922—Withdraws from Columbia University.

1923—Voyages to West Africa as merchant seaman.

1924—Lives in Paris, working as dishwasher in a jazz club.

1925—Wins first prize for poetry in *Opportunity* magazine contest.

1926—First book, *The Weary Blues*, published; enters Lincoln University.

1927—Second book of poetry, *Fine Clothes to the Jew*, published.

1929—Graduates from Lincoln University.

1930—First novel, *Not Without Laughter*, published; collaborates with Zora Neale Hurston on play *Mule Bone*.

1931—Poetry tour of the South, sponsored by Harmon Foundation.

1932—Travels to the Soviet Union as movie scriptwriter and journalist; children's books *The Dream Keeper* and *Popo and Fifina* published.

1933—Crosses Soviet Union by train and returns home via Far East and Hawaii.

1934—First book of short stories, *The Ways of White Folks*, published; father, James Hughes, dies in Mexico.

1936—*Mulatto* becomes the longest-running Broadway play by African-American author.

1937—Covers Spanish Civil War for Associated Negro Press.

1938—Founds the Suitcase Theater; mother, Carrie Clark, dies.

1940—Publishes first autobiographical volume, *The Big Sea*.

1941—Works for Writers' War Board.

1943—Creates character Jesse B. Semple for Chicago *Defender*.

1947—Broadway musical *Street Scene* debuts.

1948—Buys Harlem townhouse, his first permanent home.

1949—Teaches at Laboratory School of University of Chicago.

1950—Publishes *Simple Speaks His Mind*, his first bestseller.

1953—Ordered to testify before Senator Joseph McCarthy's congressional committee.

1956—Second volume of autobiography, *I Wonder As I Wander*, published; play *Simply Heavenly*, based on Simple stories, plays off-Broadway.

1957—Publishes *The Book of Negro Folklore* with Arna Bontemps.

1959—*Selected Poems* gathers the best of forty-eight years of published poetry.

1960—Receives the NAACP Spingarn Medal.

1961—Inducted into National Institute of Arts and Letters.

1966—Appointed official American representative to First World Festival of Negro Arts in Dakar, Senegal.

1967—Dies in New York City.

Chapter Notes

Chapter 1

1. "Langston Hughes: 45th Spingarn Medalist," *The Crisis,* August-September 1960, pp. 422–423.
2. Ibid., p. 423.
3. Ibid.
4. Ibid.
5. Arnold Rampersad, *The Life of Langston Hughes: Volume II: I Dream a World* (New York: Oxford University Press, 1988), p. 312.
6. Ibid., p. 313.
7. Langston Hughes, *The Big Sea* (New York: Hill and Wang, 1940), p. 34.
8. Rampersad, p. 312.
9. St. Clair Bourne, "George Houston Bass on Langston Hughes," *Langston Hughes Review,* vol. 9–10, 1990–1991, p. 100.

Chapter 2

1. Langston Hughes, *The Big Sea* (New York: Hill and Wang, 1940), p. 14.
2. Ibid.
3. Ibid., p. 16.
4. Arnold Rampersad, *The Life of Langston Hughes: Volume I: I, Too, Sing America* (New York: Oxford University Press, 1986), p. 14.
5. Ibid., pp. 14–15.
6. Ibid., p. 17.
7. Hughes, p. 17.
8. Rampersad, p. 24.

9. Hughes, p. 35.

Chapter 3

1. Langston Hughes, *The Big Sea* (New York: Hill and Wang, 1940), p. 36.

2. Ibid., p. 37.

3. Ibid.

4. Ibid., p. 41.

5. Ibid., p. 39.

6. Ibid., p. 40.

7. Ibid., p. 45.

8. Ibid., p. 48.

9. Arnold Rampersad, *The Life of Langston Hughes: Volume I: I, Too, Sing America* (New York: Oxford University Press, 1986), p. 34.

10. Hughes, p. 51.

11. Milton Meltzer, *Langston Hughes: A Biography* (New York: Crowell, 1968), p. 32.

12. Rampersad, p. 50.

13. Hughes, p. 55.

14. Ibid., pp. 61–62.

15. Rampersad, p. 48.

16. Hughes, p. 83.

Chapter 4

1. Langston Hughes, *The Big Sea* (New York: Hill and Wang, 1940), p. 86.

2. Ibid., p. 90.

3. Ibid., p. 11.

4. Arnold Rampersad, *The Life of Langston Hughes: Volume I: I, Too, Sing America* (New York: Oxford University Press, 1986), p. 72.

5. Hughes, p. 10.

6. Ibid., p. 102.
7. Rampersad, p. 74.
8. Hughes, p. 11.
9. Langston Hughes, *The Collected Poems of Langston Hughes* (New York: Knopf, 1994), p. 40.
10. Hughes, *The Big Sea*, p. 145.
11. Hughes, *Collected Poems*, p. 39.
12. Ibid., p. 46.

Chapter 5

1. Milton Meltzer, *Langston Hughes: A Biography* (New York: Crowell, 1968), p. 110.
2. Arna Bontemps, ed., *The Harlem Renaissance Remembered* (New York: Dodd, Mead, 1972), p. 19.
3. Ibid., p. 20.
4. David Levering Lewis, *When Harlem Was in Vogue* (New York: Oxford University Press, 1981), p. 93.
5. Ibid., p. 103.
6. Arnold Rampersad, *The Life of Langston Hughes: Volume I: I, Too, Sing America* (New York: Oxford University Press, 1986), p. 107.
7. Langston Hughes, *The Collected Poems of Langston Hughes* (New York: Knopf, 1994), p. 50.
8. Rampersad, p. 110.
9. Ibid., p. 129.
10. Meltzer, p. 123.
11. Rampersad, p. 128.
12. Hughes, p. 72.
13. Rampersad, pp. 140–141.
14. Nathan Huggins, ed., *Voices From the Harlem Renaissance* (New York: Oxford University Press, 1995), p. 305.

15. Ibid., p. 306.
16. Ibid., p. 309.
17. Rampersad, p. 141.

Chapter 6

1. Langston Hughes, *The Big Sea* (New York: Hill and Wang, 1940), p. 312.

2. Arnold Rampersad, *The Life of Langston Hughes: Volume I: I, Too, Sing America* (New York: Oxford University Press, 1986), p. 148.

3. Ibid., p. 109.
4. Hughes, p. 54.
5. Rampersad, p. 153.
6. Ibid., p. 164.
7. Ibid., p. 168.
8. Hughes, p. 308.
9. Ibid., p. 305.
10. Ibid., p. 319.
11. Ibid., p. 325.
12. Rampersad, p. 196.
13. Ibid., p. 194.
14. Langston Hughes, *I Wonder As I Wander* (New York: Rinehart and Co., Inc., 1956), p. 27.
15. Ibid., p. 3.
16. Ibid., p. 5.
17. Ibid., p. 39.
18. Ibid., p. 42.
19. Rampersad, pp. 233–234.
20. Hughes, *I Wonder As I Wander,* p. 50.

Chapter 7

1. Langston Hughes, *I Wonder As I Wander* (New York: Rinehart and Co., Inc., 1956), p. 75.

2. Arnold Rampersad, *The Life of Langston Hughes: Volume I: I, Too, Sing America* (New York: Oxford University Press, 1986), p. 249.

3. Hughes, p. 95.

4. Faith Berry, ed., *Good Morning Revolution: Uncollected Writings of Social Protest by Langston Hughes* (New York: Citadel Press, 1992), p. 81.

5. Rampersad, p. 258.

6. Berry, p. 89.

7. Ibid.

8. Si-Lan Chen Leyda, *Footnote to History* (New York: Dance Horizons, 1984), p. 162.

9. Hughes, p. 256.

Chapter 8

1. Langston Hughes, *The Collected Poems of Langston Hughes* (New York: Knopf, 1994), p. 162.

2. Arnold Rampersad, *The Life of Langston Hughes: Volume I: I, Too, Sing America* (New York: Oxford University Press, 1986), p. 286.

3. Ibid., p. 287.

4. Faith Berry, *Langston Hughes: Before and Beyond Harlem* (Westport, Conn.: Lawrence Hill, 1983), p. 277.

5. Langston Hughes, *I Wonder As I Wander* (New York: Rinehart and Co., Inc., 1956), p. 310.

6. Rampersad, p. 314.

7. Ibid., p. 319.

8. Ibid., p. 325.

9. Hughes, *Collected Poems*, p. 201.

10. Hughes, *I Wonder As I Wander,* p. 395.

11. Ibid., p. 400.

Chapter 9

1. Arnold Rampersad, *The Life of Langston Hughes: Volume II: I Dream a World* (New York: Oxford University Press, 1988), p. 53.

2. Langston Hughes, *The Collected Poems of Langston Hughes* (New York: Knopf, 1994), p. 240.

3. Rampersad, p. 109.

4. James A. Emanuel, *Langston Hughes* (New York: Twayne, 1967) p. 163.

5. Eloise McKinney Johnson, "Remembering Langston Hughes: Memories of a Langston Hughes Class," *Langston Hughes Review*, vol. 7, Spring 1988, p. 35.

6. Charles H. Nichols, ed., *Arna Bontemps–Langston Hughes Letters: 1925–1967* (New York: Dodd, Mead, 1980), p. 256.

7. Hughes, p. 358.

8. Ibid., from "Harlem," p. 426

Chapter 10

1. Arnold Rampersad, *The Life of Langston Hughes: Volume II: I Dream a World* (New York: Oxford University Press, 1988), p. 204.

2. Ibid., pp. 215–217.

3. Ibid., p. 219.

4. John Henrik Clarke, ed., *Harlem: A Community in Transition* (New York: Citadel Press, 1964), p. 62.

5. George Houston Bass, "Five Stories About a Man Named Hughes: A Critical Reflection," *Langston Hughes Review*, vol. 1, Spring 1982, p. 6.

6. Charles H. Nichols, ed., *Arna Bontemps–Langston Hughes Letters: 1925–1967* (New York: Dodd, Mead, 1980), p. 486.

7. Rampersad, p. 309.

8. Jean Blackwell Hutson, as told to Jill Nelson, "Remembering Langston," *Essence*, February 1992, p. 96.

Chapter 11

1. Langston Hughes, *The Collected Poems of Langston Hughes* (New York: Knopf, 1994), p. 501.

2. Arnold Rampersad, *The Life of Langston Hughes: Volume II: I Dream a World* (New York: Oxford University Press, 1988), p. 328.

3. Ibid., p. 362.

4. Ibid., p. 399.

5. Ibid., p. 403.

6. Ibid., pp. 337–338.

7. Ibid., p. 150.

8. Charles H. Nichols, ed., *Arna Bontemps–Langston Hughes Letters: 1925–1967* (New York: Dodd, Mead, 1980), p. 468.

9. Rampersad, p. 373.

10. George Houston Bass, "Five Stories About a Man Named Hughes: A Critical Reflection," *Langston Hughes Review*, vol. 1, Spring 1982, p. 100.

11. St. Clair Bourne, "George Houston Bass on Langston Hughes," *Langston Hughes Review*, vol. 9–10, 1990–1991, p. 100.

12. Rampersad, p. 419.

13. Bass, p. 4.

14. Gwendolyn Brooks, *Report from Part One* (Detroit: Broadside Press, 1972), p. 70.

15. Hughes, p. 547.

16. "The Living Langston," *Ebony*, May 1991, p. 82.

FURTHER READING

Haskins, James. *The Harlem Renaissance.* Brookfield, Conn.: Millbrook Press, 1996.

Hughes, Langston. *The Best of Simple.* New York: Farrar, Straus & Giroux, 1990.

———. *The Big Sea.* New York: Hill & Wang, 1993.

———. *The Collected Poems of Langston Hughes.* New York: Knopf, 1994.

———. *The Collected Stories of Langston Hughes.* New York: Hill & Wang, 1996.

———. *The Dream Keeper.* New York: Knopf, 1994.

———. *I Wonder As I Wander.* New York: Hill & Wang, 1993.

———. *Not Without Laughter.* New York: Macmillan, 1986.

———, and Arna Bontemps. *Popo and Fifina.* New York: Oxford University Press, 1993.

———, and Zora Neale Hurston. *Mule Bone: A Comedy of Negro Life in Three Acts.* New York: HarperCollins Publishers, 1991.

Meltzer, Milton. *Langston Hughes: A Biography.* New York: Crowell, 1968.

Osofsky, Audrey. *Free to Dream, the Making of a Poet: Langston Hughes.* New York: Lothrop, Lee & Shepard, 1996.

Rampersad, Arnold. *The Life of Langston Hughes: Vol. I: 1902–1941: I, Too, Sing America.* New York: Oxford University Press, 1986.

———. *The Life of Langston Hughes: Vol. II: 1941–1967: I Dream a World.* New York: Oxford University Press, 1988.

Watson, Steven. *The Harlem Renaissance: Hub of African-American Culture, 1920–1930.* New York: Pantheon, 1995.

INDEX